The Apos

The Apostle Question

*

Exploring the Roles of Apostles in the New Testament Church

Written by: Prophet Roderick L. Evans

Kingdom Builders
PUBLISHING

CAMDEN, NORTH CAROLINA

The Apostle Question
Exploring the Role of Apostles in the New Testament Church

Front & Back Cover Designs by Kingdom Builders Publishing
Images developed from Microsoft Clip Art & Media
Copyright © 2004 Microsoft Corporation, One Microsoft Way,
Redmond, Washington 98052-6399
U.S.A. All rights reserved.

Kingdom Builders Publishing
an imprint of Kingdom Builders International Ministries

For information address:
Kingdom Builders International
P.O. Box 126
Camden, NC 27921

Unless otherwise indicated, all of the scripture quotations are taken from the *Authorized King James Version* **of the Bible. Scripture quotations marked with NIV are taken from the** *New International Version* **of the Bible. Scripture quotations marked with NASV are taken from the** *New American Standard Version* **of the Bible. Scripture quotations marked with Amplified are taken from the** *Amplified Bible.*

ISBN: 978-1-60141-007-8

Printed in the United States of America

Contents

Preface

Introduction

Chapter 1 – What is an Apostle?   **1**

    Apostolic Ministry in the Old Testament   *2*
    Apostolic Ministry in the New Testament   *5*

Chapter 2 – The Call of an Apostle   **11**

    Acknowledging the Apostolic Call   *12*
    Answering the Apostolic Call   *15*
    Accepting the Apostolic Call   *19*

Chapter 3 – The Making of an Apostle   **23**

    Marring of the Apostle   *24*
    Love of the Apostle   *26*
    Building of the Apostle   *29*
    The Apostle's Character   *34*

Chapter 4 – The Office of the Apostle   **41**

    Apostles as Ambassadors   *41*
    Apostles as Fathers   *45*
    Nine Functions of the Apostle   *50*
    Focus of Apostles   *54*

Chapter 5 – The Apostolic Person   **57**

    The Apostolic Person is a Disciple   *58*
    The Apostolic Person is a Son   *59*
    The Apostolic Person is a Brother   *60*
    The Apostolic Person's Character   *61*
    Recognizing the Apostolic Person   *63*
    Flowing as an Apostolic Person   *66*

Chapter 6 – Apostles in Perspective   **69**

    Apostles and the Church   *69*
    Apostles and Pastors   *73*
    Apostles versus Prophets   *75*
    Misconceptions   *76*

Chapter 7 – What is Apostleship?   **85**

    The Apostolic Gift   *86*
    The Apostolic Anointing   *87*
    The Apostolic Spirit   *88*
    Guidelines for Judging the Apostolic   *93*

Chapter 8 – False Apostles   **97**

    Recognizing False Ministers   *98*
    Recognizing False Apostles   *101*

About the Author   105

Appendix   **107**

Bibliography   111

Other Books

Preface

Apostles and apostolic ministry are important to the furtherance of the Kingdom of God and the Church. It is my prayer that the information presented in this work will bring clarity, appreciation, and understanding to apostles and apostolic ministry.

Numerous works have been produced which highlight the ministry of the apostle. This book is to be used in connection with other publications. It is our prayer that those called to this office will gain insight for their ministries. In addition, I pray that others will develop an understanding of this ministry in the Church.

Roderick L. Evans

Introduction

Controversy over the gifts and ministries of the Spirit has abounded for centuries. Various scholars have taught that there was a cessation of the gifts and ministries. More specifically, they affirm that the ministry of the Apostle is no longer in operation nor valid. However, in recent years, a resurgence of the operation and demonstration of this ministry occurred. Traditional and Non-traditional churches, alike, have experienced the visitation of God through the Holy Spirit.

Since the emergence and acceptance of the ministries and gifts of the Holy Spirit, various authors have written concerning this phenomenon. In spite of this, many in the Church, presently, do not understand the functions and operations of, namely, the office of the Apostle. Even in organizations and denominations that consider this ministry valid today, comprehension is oftentimes elementary.

Where there is no clear understanding, individuals become vulnerable to deception and error. Since the apostolic office has authority and responsibility in the Kingdom of God, there are individuals in the Church who desire to function in this office. There are men and women who know they are not called to this office, yet they pursue it. They lust after the respect that men have for those in this office. If they cannot be recognized as an apostle, some want to be identified with the office. Therefore, individuals resort to saying that they have an apostolic anointing upon their lives, without having any knowledge or understanding of the office or the anointing associated with it.

In this book, we will bring clarity to the role of the apostle in the New Testament Church. In addition, we will explain with simplicity the apostolic anointing. It is our prayer that believers will recognize the operation of this anointing in their lives and in the lives of others. We can be confident that God is still using His people in these last days.

1

What is an Apostle?

The first ministry to be on display in the New Testament Church was that of the apostle. The Book of Acts highlights the ministry of the apostles. Some biblical scholars have asserted that the only true apostles were the eleven disciples (excluding Judas Iscariot) with the exception of Paul. Others have stated that the ministry of the apostles is useless since we have the canon of scripture.

In addition, others promote that apostolic ministry ceased after the deaths of the first century apostles. As believers, we must understand that these teachings are erroneous. ***The ministry of the apostle is still vital and important to the advancement of the kingdom of God and the Church.*** Without this ministry, the Church cannot fulfill its mission in the earth.

> *And He set some in the Church, first apostles..*
> *(I Corinthians 12:28)*

1

The word apostle originates from the Greek word *apostolos,* which means one who is sent forth. Apostles are sent from the presence of God with a divine message. They are sent forth for a specific task. Not all apostles will discharge their duty in the same manner; neither will they all have the same anointing.

Apostles' ministries will vary in demonstration and execution. Though apostolic ministry seems exclusive to the New Testament, we discover from the scriptures that apostolic ministry was demonstrated in the Old Testament.

Apostolic Ministry in the Old Testament

The apostolic ministry is a foundational ministry (will be discussed later). The apostolic anointing is designed to bring people into the knowledge of God and Christ. In the Old Testament, some men seemed to have an apostolic grace upon their lives.

Two key biblical figures that exemplify this truth are Abraham and Moses. Each of these men were prophets, but from God's interaction with them, we discover there was a type of apostolic anointing on their lives. They demonstrated three apostolic traits:

1) They reflect the character of God.
2) They established individuals in the faith of God.
3) They exercised great spiritual authority and power.

2

Abraham was sent to a foreign land by the command of God. Abraham received a commission as does an apostle.

> *Now the Lord had said unto Abram, Get thee out of thy country, and from thy kindred, and from thy father's house, unto a land that I will shew thee. (Genesis 12:1)*

The apostolic grace was evident in Abraham's life because it was through his life that foreigners were introduced to the God of heaven. The Lord magnified Himself in Abraham's life as he traveled throughout the land. We know that *Abraham's character reflected God's* as the apostle's does Christ. For God commanded him saying,

> *And when Abram was ninety years old and nine, the Lord appeared to Abram, and said unto him, I am the Almighty God; walk before me, and be thou perfect. (Genesis 17:1)*

Like the modern day apostle, *Abraham was used to establish the faith of God* in his descendants and in the earth. As apostles are fathers in the Spirit, Abraham is the father of faith.

> *And God said unto Abraham, Thou shalt keep my covenant therefore, thou, and thy seed after thee in their generations. (Genesis 17:9)*

Finally, Abraham exercised great authority and power.

3

After God rebuked Abimelech for Sarah's sake, He told the king that Abraham would pray for him and the barrenness of his household would end. As apostles exercise great power, so did Abraham through his prayer.

> *So Abraham prayed unto God: and God healed Abimelech, and his wife, and his maidservants; and they bare children. For the Lord had fast closed up all the wombs of the house of Abimelech, because of Sarah Abraham's wife. (Genesis 20;17-18)*

Moses, like Abraham demonstrated apostolic grace. When God spoke of his ministry, He said that Moses was not like other prophets. *Apostles and prophets are similar, but the apostle's ministry is greater than the prophet's because of the spiritual authority of the office.* This is what Moses represented in his day. He was a prophet, but there was something greater about him.

> *And he said, Hear now my words: If there be a prophet among you, I the Lord will make myself known unto him in a vision, and will speak unto him in a dream. My servant Moses is not so, who is faithful in all mine house. (Numbers 12:6-7)*

When God sent Moses to Pharaoh, He told Moses that Aaron would be his prophet, and Moses would be as God to Pharaoh. This is a clear demonstration of the apostolic grace. Moses would reflect God's character as he fulfilled his ministry. Numerous biblical accounts recall the power that Moses exercised. Signs and wonders surrounded his ministry to the Jews. This is parallel to the ministry of the apostles.

Finally, like the modern day apostle, Moses established people in the faith of God. The apostles laid a spiritual foundation for the Church to grow upon while Moses instituted the Law from God to set up the Levitical priesthood and Israelite worship.

From these two patriarchs, we see a demonstration and foreshadowing of the apostolic ministry to come under the New Covenant.

Apostolic Ministry in the New Testament

After the establishment of the Church, God used apostles. ***The apostle is sent as a chief representative of Christ.*** They represent the person of Christ to the Church and world (however, this is done alongside other believers and ministers). They are preachers of the Gospel of Jesus Christ.

Apostles mature believers in their walks with the Lord. They serve as spiritual fathers. They have the grace upon their lives to establish order to the worship of God. In addition, they have prophetic insight and great authority in the realm of the Spirit.

In addition to the above functions, the New

5

Testament apostle serves as a foundational ministry to the Church. On the day of Pentecost, God established His will for man's worship. He no longer wanted to be "confined" to a building (represented by God's command to worship at the Temple), but dwell in the hearts of man. His will was for the believer to be His temple.

As He abides in each individual, they corporately become the temple of God. Peter called the believers "stones" who are built together to form a spiritual house or temple where God could dwell.

> *Ye also, as lively stones, are built up a spiritual house, an holy priesthood, to offer up spiritual sacrifices, acceptable to God by Jesus Christ. (I Peter 2:5)*

> *What? Know ye not that your body is the temple of the Holy Ghost which is in you, which ye have of God, and ye are not your own? (I Corinthians 6:19)*

With the New Covenant, the temple of God is now the hearts and minds of people. Their actual bodies become the habitation of God. Therefore, if the Church consists of people joined together by the presence of the Holy Spirit, then the foundation for the Church would consist of people.

As Paul wrote to the believers, he revealed to them a very important truth. He told them that they (the Church) were built upon the foundation of the **apostles** and prophets with Christ being the head stone.

> *Now therefore ye are no more strangers and foreigners, but fellowcitizens with the saints, and of the household of God; And are built upon the foundation of the apostles and prophets, Jesus Christ himself being the chief corner stone; In whom all the building fitly framed together groweth unto an holy temple in the Lord: In whom ye also are builded together for an habitation of God through the Spirit. (Ephesians 2:19-22).*

In the above scripture, we discover certain truths. Paul was writing to a primarily Gentile audience. However, we must understand that the foundation that they stood upon was the same as the Jewish believers. Jewish and Gentile believers, alike, operated in the foundation established by the New Testament **apostles** and prophets.

The Church, like the New Covenant, was founded upon people, namely, the **apostles** and prophets. From this, we understand that since we will reign with Christ, God allowed man to have an active role in the establishment of the Church.

The **apostles** and prophets bear the responsibility for the Church, especially in doctrinal purity and spiritual direction. As Christ formed the

7

foundation for the New Covenant, the **apostles** and prophets formed the foundation for the Church.

Their ministries are foundational and continue to be major influences upon the Body of Christ.

The ministries of the **apostles** and prophets were needed to establish the Church, and their ministries are needed presently for the furtherance of the Church. Christ's ministry toward us is everlasting.

> *But this man, because he continueth ever, hath an unchangeable priesthood. Wherefore he is able also to save them to the uttermost that come unto God by him, seeing he ever liveth to make intercession for them. (Hebrews 7:24-25)*

The Book of Acts reveals to us that the ministries of the apostles were essential in the establishment of the Church and the advancement of the Kingdom of God.

Consider the following:

Signs and wonders accompanied the apostles' ministries to confirm the message that they preached. This helps to advance the Kingdom of God.

> *And fear came upon every soul: and many wonders and signs were done by the apostles. (Acts 2:43)*

God also bearing them witness, both with signs and wonders, and with divers miracles, and gifts of the Holy Ghost, according to his own will. (Hebrews 2:4)

The apostles' ministries were vital to establishing the Church and believers in the faith.

And they continued stedfastly in the apostles' doctrine and fellowship, and in breaking of bread, and in prayers. (Acts 2:42)

This second epistle, beloved, I now write unto you; in both which I stir up your pure minds by way of remembrance: That ye may be mindful of the words which were spoken before by the holy prophets, and of the commandment of us the apostles of the Lord and Saviour. (2 Peter 3:1-2)

Not only did the New Testament apostles reveal future events and encourage the brethren, but also they helped to set up elders and pastors in the Church.

For this cause left I thee in Crete, that thou shouldest set in order the things that are wanting, and ordain elders in every city, as I had appointed thee. (Titus 1:5)

From the above scriptures and references, we discover that the New Testament Church has apostles, individuals who possess as apostolic anointing, and

9

those who have and apostolic gift. These gifts were needed then and they are needed now.

There are some theologians who twist the scriptures. They assert that because we have the canon of scripture, apostles and apostolic ministry are no longer needed. The scriptures declare that Jesus Christ is the same yesterday, today, and forever (Hebrews 13:8). He ministered to the early Church through the apostles. He will not change until the end of all things.

If He used apostles and apostolic ministry in those times, He will continue to do so. Christ's ministry to the Church will not end until the Judgment; therefore, the ministries of the apostles will not end until that Day. God is still using apostles today. In addition, God is raising up individuals who walk under and in an apostolic anointing that His glory may be seen in all.

2

The Call of an Apostle

God calls individuals to the apostolic office in many ways. In the Old and New Testaments, we discover that God called men in different manners. God's call to the apostolic office is an undeniable call. The apostle's ministry is needed if the Church is going to mature and the Kingdom of God is to advance. Therefore, God establishes them in their work through His calling. There are individuals calling themselves apostles without having a definite call from the Lord or confirmation from among the brethren.

This chapter is designed to help believers recognize the apostolic calling upon others and themselves. We will look at scriptural examples of how the Lord called individuals to understand the call of the apostle.

Acknowledging the Apostolic Call

The call of an apostle is unique from others in one respect. Though all ministers receive their calling from the Lord, the apostolic call comes with a revelation of Christ. Since the New Testament highlights the ministry of the apostles, we will use examples from these texts to understand the apostle's call.

Jesus & the Twelve

After His ministry began, Jesus called men to walk aside Him. These men were later called apostles.

> *And when it was day, he called unto him his disciples: and of them he chose twelve, whom also he named apostles. (Luke 6:13)*

This verse gives us an extremely important truth concerning apostles. ***ONLY JESUS CAN CALL APOSTLES.*** Serving an apostle does not make one a candidate for this ministry. A prophetic word does not make one an apostle, except it is truly from the Lord.

Desiring this office greatly does not signify a call to this office. Jesus will call and ordain apostles personally. After His calling, there will be confirmation of it in the Church.

In the book of John, we discover that after John the Baptist revealed whom Christ was, two of his disciples left to follow Jesus.

> *Again the next day after John stood, and two of his disciples; And looking upon Jesus as he*

> *walked, he saith, Behold the Lamb of God!*
> *And the two disciples heard him speak, and*
> *they followed Jesus. (John 1:35-37)*

The apostolic call does not begin with the apostle
fulfilling a ministry, but it begins with a revelation of
Jesus. When John and Andrew discovered who Christ
was, they immediately followed Him. Jesus did not
call them, but they pursued.

Individuals who are called to the apostleship
usually are concerned with following and pleasing
Christ above a calling to a ministry. This is a part of
their calling. If they cannot follow the person of Christ,
they will not be able to represent Him, as they should
in ministry. The apostle's call normally begins with an
inward conviction and witness before an external
experience is given.

Continuing our examination of the twelve, we
discover that Jesus called them personally also.

> *And going on from thence, he saw other two*
> *brethren, James the son of Zebedee, and John*
> *his brother, in a ship with Zebedee their*
> *father, mending their nets; and he called them.*
> *And they immediately left the ship and their*
> *father, and followed him. (Matthew 4:18-22)*
>
> *And as he passed by, he saw Levi the son of*
> *Alphaeus sitting at the receipt of custom, and*

said unto him, Follow me. And he arose and
followed him. (Mark 2:14)

The apostle's call will be a personal one. He will be
brought face to face with Jesus Christ. The apostle's
call begins with a revelation of Jesus and then a time
of following Him in service. The apostles followed
Him and ministered unto Him before they operated in
full apostolic authority. *Any individual claiming to*
have an apostolic call without a servant's heart is
probably not called of God. The apostles willingly
served Jesus.

When we consider the conversion of Saul, we
discover that Jesus called Him in a similar manner.
Before He received His calling, he received a personal
encounter and revelation of Jesus.

> *And he fell to the earth, and heard a voice*
> *saying unto him, Saul, Saul, why persecutest*
> *thou me? And he said, Who art thou, Lord?*
> *And the Lord said, I am Jesus whom thou*
> *persecutest: it is hard for thee to kick against*
> *the pricks. And he trembling and astonished*
> *said, Lord, what wilt thou have me to do? And*
> *the Lord said unto him, Arise, and go into the*
> *city, and it shall be told thee what thou must*
> *do. (Acts 9:4-6)*

Because of the future apostolic ministry, we find that
Saul's response to the Lord was like the other apostles.
After Jesus told Him who He was, his next response

was an inquiry, as to what the Lord wanted Him to do. Saul did not wrestle or fight, he immediately expressed his desire to obey and follow Christ. After demonstrating his willingness to follow Him, Saul received an understanding and confirmation of his call to ministry.

> *And one Ananias, a devout man according to the law, having a good report of all the Jews which dwelt there, Came unto me, and stood, and said unto me, Brother Saul, receive thy sight. And the same hour I looked up upon him. And he said, The God of our fathers hath chosen thee, that thou shouldest know his will, and see that Just One, and shouldest hear the voice of his mouth. For thou shalt be his witness unto all men of what thou hast seen and heard. (Acts 22:12-15)*

The modern day apostle's calling will come in a similar manner. He will be consumed with following Christ. As a result, he will experience an encounter with the Lord that will substantiate his ministry. After these things, there will be confirmation through the brethren.

Answering the Apostolic Call

Once an individual receives a call to the apostolic office, there must be a response and answer to the Lord. Before the apostle's making (discussed in the next chapter) begins, there are certain things that the future apostle has to do.

15

Seek Servant-hood

The apostle's office comes with great authority and power. The apostle has to guard his spirit against arrogance and pride. A sure of way of this is to develop a servant's heart. He should seek opportunities to serve. Since apostles are called at different times in their lives and ministries, this can be difficult.

> *But he that is greatest among you shall be your servant. (Matthew 23:11)*

Some individuals receive a call to the apostolic office after being in ministry for years. In this instance, the individual needs to find someone they can submit to and serve in order to prepare for the budding apostolic ministry. Jesus demonstrated the level of humility that an apostle needs when He washed the disciples' feet.

> *So after he had washed their feet, and had taken his garments, and was set down again, he said unto them, Know ye what I have done to you? Ye call me Master and Lord: and ye say well; for so I am. If I then, your Lord and Master, have washed your feet; ye also ought to wash one another's feet. For I have given you an example, that ye should do as I have done to you. (John 13:12-15)*

Jesus showed the apostles that even though they would have great power and authority, they should be willing

16

to serve even in the lowest forms. The apostles received this lesson well.

Even after Pentecost and expansion of the Church through their miraculous ministry, the apostles still served food to the widows (Acts 6:1-8). Though they healed the sick, raised the dead, and preached the Gospel, they were still servants. It was only after the service hindered their ministry that they appointed others to serve the widows for them.

Seek Solitude

After receiving notice of a call to the apostolic, a time of separation is needed to ensure the apostle's success. The separation does not necessarily have to be physical, but definitely spiritual. The apostle has to take time to seek the Lord and receive revelation from Jesus concerning His Church.

After his conversion and calling, Paul experienced a time of separation in order to be instructed of the Lord.

> ***But when it pleased God, who separated me from my mother's womb, and called me by his grace, To reveal his Son in me, that I might preach him among the heathen; immediately I conferred not with flesh and blood: Neither went I up to Jerusalem to them which were apostles before me; but I went into Arabia, and returned again unto Damascus. Then after three years I went up to Jerusalem to see***

*Peter, and abode with him fifteen days.
(Galatians 1:15-18)*

Paul wrote that when God wanted to reveal Christ to him, he went into Arabia and then Damascus over the space of three years. He wrote that he did not discuss it with men, he allowed the Lord to minister unto him. After the Lord was finished, Paul spoke to other apostles to verify the things he had received.

The modern day apostle will be called into a time of solitude with the Lord. During this time, the Lord will correct erroneous beliefs and doctrines so that the apostle can fully reflect Christ in his doctrine and ministry. *The information that the apostle receives during this time will not divide the Church or be "brand new."*

When Paul conferred with the other apostles, they verified that the things he preached were of the Lord. God will confirm the apostle's revelation (usually through other apostles).

Seek Sanctification

A call to the apostolic office is an invitation to spiritual warfare. If the enemy cannot stop the individual's resolve to serve the Lord, he will weaken the future apostle's ministry through ungodliness. Therefore, the apostle has to seek sanctification; that is, a life of holiness to ensure success in the ministry.

> ***But I keep under my body, and bring it into
> subjection: lest that by any means, when I
> have preached to others, I myself should be a
> castaway. (I Corinthians 9:27)***

Paul, after years of ministry, confessed that he still had
to bring his body (flesh and its lusts) under subjection.
The apostle's quest for holiness **increases** at the
reception of his calling and **continues** during its
fulfillment.

Accepting the Apostolic Call

Since the apostolic office invites controversy,
there is confusion as to how to recognize and accept
the apostolic calling in our lives and in the lives of
others. Therefore, in concluding our examination of
the call of an apostle, we will discuss briefly certain
signs of the apostolic calling. This will help in the
acceptance of the apostolic call on an individual's life.

Revelation of Jesus Christ

The individual who is called to the apostolic
office will have a profound understanding of Jesus
Christ. He will speak of Christ in the most personal
terms. Christ will reveal Himself to the apostolic
individual through dreams and visions, through the
voice of the Spirit, or through the scriptures.
Regardless of the method used, the apostolic
individual will have a clear revelation of Christ and
His work.

> *Am I not an apostle? am I not free? have I not seen Jesus Christ our Lord? are not ye my work in the Lord? (I Corinthians 9:1)*

We must remember that all believers are to know Christ. God will reveal a deep understanding of Christ to whom He will. Though the apostle will have this level of understanding, any believer is a candidate for it. Again, this is given as a sign of a call to the apostolic office.

Consistent Intercession

Apostles have a deep love for Christ and the Church. Because of this, those who are called to this office will have consistent prayer lives. Much of their prayer will be for the Church, its members, and its advancement. They have a desire to see Christ's rule in the earth. In his letters, the apostle Paul would tell the churches of his constant intercession for them. This is a sure sign of the apostolic calling.

> *For this cause we also, since the day we heard it, do not cease to pray for you, and to desire that ye might be filled with the knowledge of his will in all wisdom and spiritual understanding. (Colossians 1:9)*

Conversely, we know that Jesus challenges all believers to be consistent in prayer. In addition, the scriptures continually admonish believers to be intercessors for one another. Again, consistent intercession may be a sign of the apostolic office, not the manifestation of it.

Authority in the Spirit

One of the sure signs of an apostolic call is the presence of great authority in the Spirit. Those who called to the apostolic office will have the revelation gifts of the Spirit operating in them consistently. In addition, they will possess the power gifts of healing and working of miracles. They will be effective in the casting out of demons.

> **Truly the signs of an apostle were wrought among you in all patience, in signs, and wonders, and mighty deeds. (2 Corinthians 12:12)**

The revelation and power of the Spirit is available to all Christians. Jesus said that miraculous signs would follow anyone who believed on Him. Therefore, it is not uncommon to see believers who are not called to the apostolic possessing great power and authority.

The presence of power and authority, again, is only a sign of the apostolic call. We have already established that **ONLY JESUS CAN CALL APOSTLES.** The above signs are only indications of an apostolic call.

Once an apostolic call is established, the apostle goes through training and discipline. In the next chapter, we will discuss the making of an apostle. Exercising great power and authority in the Spirit is not the hallmark of the apostle's ministry; it is his character. Therefore, Christ builds the apostle to reflect His nature.

3

The Making of an Apostle

The apostle's ministry comes with authority, power, and the miraculous. This is only a part of the apostle's ministry. His ministry serves as a reflection of Christ's ministry to the Church. Therefore, the apostle's character has to be solid. Therefore, God will take the apostles through tests, trials, and temptations in order to prepare them for ministry.

The training of an apostle is oftentimes humiliating. God will allow disruption in every area of his life to prepare him for service. Those called to the apostolic office should understand that preparation for ministry is in the development of Christ's character. If this is done, the apostle will never come behind in any spiritual gift during ministry.

In this chapter, we will discuss how God builds the apostle for ministry.

Marring of the Apostle: *Jeremiah's girdle*

Jeremiah prophesied to Judah during a time of great rebellion and sin against God. To express His judgment upon Judah, God instructed Jeremiah to hide his girdle in a rock and leave it for a length of time.

> *And the word of the Lord came unto me the second time, saying, Take the girdle that thou hast got, which is upon thy loins, and arise, go to Euphrates, and hide it there in a hole of the rock. So I went, and hid it by Euphrates, as the Lord commanded me. And it came to pass after many days, that the Lord said unto me, Arise, go to Euphrates, and take the girdle from thence, which I commanded thee to hide there. Then I went to Euphrates, and digged, and took the girdle from the place where I had hid it: and, behold, the girdle was marred, it was profitable for nothing. (Jeremiah 13:3-7)*

Jeremiah's girdle was marred. When something is marred, it is ruined. Jeremiah's girdle had decayed. In the following verses, God said that He would mar Jerusalem and Judah's pride. This is what the Lord does to the apostle. *An apostle has to recognize that he is nothing without God.* Therefore, God will allow the apostle to experience embarrassment and humiliation to prepare him for the authority that is before him.

Without understanding his position before God, the apostle will fall into pride and arrogance. Thus, God breaks him down in order to preserve him.

> *I am become a fool in glorying; ye have compelled me: for I ought to have been commended of you: for in nothing am I behind the very chiefest apostles, though I be nothing. (2 Corinthians 12:11)*

Paul spoke of his ministry, but declared he was nothing. Because of God's discipline and training, Paul walked in humility even after years of powerful ministry.

Apostles will suffer greatly before and during ministry. God allows a continual marring process in their lives to keep them humble and broken before him.

> *For I think that God hath set forth us the apostles last, as it were appointed to death: for we are made a spectacle unto the world, and to angels, and to men. (I Corinthians 4:9)*

Because of the Lord's process, Paul stated that he felt as if apostles were appointed unto death. This means that the apostle will meet consistent opposition and tests. Those called to the apostolic office will have testimonies of great rejection, times of poverty, and sickness. They will be the subject of gossip, debate, and slander.

25

Apostles usually experience embarrassing situations to produce selflessness and humility. These things will happen even after they enter into ministry. There is a consistent call to self-death laid on the apostle. His pride will consistently be marred so that Christ and the Church may shine.

> *We are fools for Christ's sake, but ye are wise in Christ; we are weak, but ye are strong; ye are honourable, but we are despised.*
> *(I Corinthians 4:10)*

The apostle's self-death results in a fruitful ministry and healthy Church.

> *Verily, verily, I say unto you, Except a corn of wheat fall into the ground and die, it abideth alone: but if it die, it bringeth forth much fruit.*
> *(John 12:24)*

Love of the Apostle: Husbands and Wives

Part of the apostle's making is in the area of love. God places a deep love in the apostle for Christ and the Church. *If the apostle's love does not mirror Christ's, he will wreak havoc in the Church. He will damage God's people.* Since apostles stand in Christ's stead, it is important to understand that the Christ-Church relationship is marriage.

As Christ is married to the Church, so are the apostles. Husbands are to love their wives as Christ

26

loved the Church. The apostle, then, acts as a husband to the Church.

The scriptures give guidelines for how the husband is to treat his wife (Ephesians 5:22-32; I Peter 3:7). The same principles apply to the apostle.

Husbands must love their wives

Apostles have a deep love for the Church. They minister in the Church with the love and compassion of Christ. Paul instructs husbands to love and lay down their lives for their wives as Christ did for the Church. The apostle's life and ministry are set-aside for the Church and the advancement of the Kingdom of God.

The scriptures tell us that Jesus became sin for us. He loved us so much that He became a curse in the eyes of man that we may live. In the above verses, Paul gives an account to the Corinthian Church of how they are suffering many things for their sakes.

Apostles are to lay down their lives for the Church, that the glory of God may be seen in her, Jesus said.

> *Greater love hath no man than this, that a man lay down his life for his friends. (John 15:13)*

The greatest demonstration of love by Christ was that He gave His life for us. The apostle has to be willing to do the same for the Church.

Husbands must impart the Word to their wives

As Christ sanctified the Church by the Word, so should husbands be able to impart life to their wives by the Word. As husbands to the Church, apostles share in the responsibility of cleansing the Church through the Word, that she may be presented unto God without spot or winkle.

The focus of the apostle's ministry is to make ready a people for the coming of the Lord, and to present the Church to Christ as a chaste bride. This is accomplished through the preaching of the Word. Consider the following:

> *Now ye are clean through the word which I have spoken unto you. (John 15:3)*

> *For I am jealous over you with godly jealousy: for I have espoused you to one husband, that I may present you as a chaste virgin to Christ. (II Corinthians 11:2)*

Jesus pronounced His disciples clean because He had preached the Word unto them. The apostle, like Christ, cleanses the Church through the Word.

Husbands must love their wives as their own bodies.

Husbands are instructed to love their wives as their own bodies. Apostles have to minister with great

28

love. Though they minister to the Church, they themselves are also a part of the Church. Husbands are admonished to nourish and cherish their wives as they would their own bodies. Apostles should remember to minister to the Church as if they are ministering to themselves. The apostles and the Church will stand before the judgment seat of God.

Building of the Apostle: Christ in Revelation

God develops humility and love in the apostle to build them into fruitful ambassadors. There are general characteristics that every apostle possesses as a result of Christ's building process. Since the apostle will reflect Christ, Christ is God's prototype for building the apostle. John's vision of Christ in the book of Revelation gives a clear depiction of how God builds the apostle.

> *And in the midst of the seven candlesticks one like unto the Son of man, clothed with a garment down to the foot, and girt about the paps with a golden girdle. His head and his hairs were white like wool, as white as snow; and his eyes were as a flame of fire; And his feet like unto fine brass, as if they burned in a furnace; and his voice as the sound of many waters. And he had in his right hand seven stars: and out of his mouth went a sharp two-edged sword: and his countenance was as the sun shineth in his strength. (Revelation 1:12-16)*

Clothed with Linen Garment & Golden Belt

The garments in the vision reflect the apostle's total consecration to God in ministry. In the Old Testament, the priests wore special garments to reflect their ministry.

The apostolic ministry is given to the Church as the priests were given to minister daily to the whole nation. The linen reflects the purity that the apostle should have in ministry, while the gold belt is representative of the truth that he will carry.

> *And thou shalt speak unto all that are wise hearted, whom I have filled with the spirit of wisdom, that they may make Aaron's garments to consecrate him, that he may minister unto me in the priest's office. (Exodus 28:3)*

Head and Hair White like Wool

The white head and hair represents the wisdom and understanding that the apostle possesses. The apostles are stewards over the mysteries of God. The Lord will give them understanding of the deep things of God. Their doctrine will be sound, being able to mature the saints.

> *Let a man so account of us, as of the ministers of Christ, and stewards of the mysteries of God. (I Corinthians 4:1)*

Eyes as a Flame of Fire

The eyes of fire reflect the apostle's spiritual insight. It also represents the apostle's ability to see into the realm of the Spirit. The apostle will not only have revelation of the scriptures, but also have prophetic insight to enhance their ministries.

> *Which in other ages was not made known unto the sons of men, as it is now revealed unto his holy apostles and prophets by the Spirit. (Ephesians 3:5)*

Feet like Fine Brass

Feet like fine brass reflect the apostle's motivation in ministry. The feet carry us from one place to another. The Lord purifies the apostle's motivation in ministry that he will continually follow Christ. This is reflected in the brass feet being burned in the furnace.

> *I am crucified with Christ: nevertheless I live; yet not I, but Christ liveth in me: and the life which I now live in the flesh I live by the faith of the Son of God, who loved me, and gave himself for me. (Galatians 2:20)*

In addition, the brass feet burned in a furnace reflects the zeal the apostle has for the Kingdom of God and the Church.

31

Voice like Many Waters

The voice like many waters reflects the soundness of speech the apostle has. The apostle will have understanding and the ability to communicate it.

> *But we speak the wisdom of God in a mystery, even the hidden wisdom, which God ordained before the world unto our glory. (I Corinthians 2:7)*

In addition, the voice of many waters represents the scope of the apostle's ministry. His word will be to the Church as a whole. The apostle will be able to reach different kinds of peoples and nationalities (the many waters) with the message of the Kingdom of God.

Seven Stars in Hand

The stars in the vision represented the seven churches. This reflects the apostle's responsibility to minister to the Church. His volition is the Church and the advancement of the Kingdom. It also reflects the apostle's influence on the Church. The apostle has the Church's direction and growth in his hand through ministry.

> *That ye may be mindful of the words which were spoken before by the holy prophets, and of the commandment of us the apostles of the Lord and Saviour. (2 Peter 3:2)*

Two-edged Sword in Mouth

The sword in the mouth reflects the effectiveness of the apostle's preaching and teaching ministry. Their words will be able to cut to the heart and produce conviction in the listeners. In addition, their words will inspire growth in the hearers. Their words will cut off "excess" that comes with religion to present Christ.

> *For the word of God is quick, and powerful, and sharper than any two-edged sword, piercing even to the dividing asunder of soul and spirit, and of the joints and marrow, and is a discerner of the thoughts and intents of the heart. (Hebrews 4:12)*

Countenance of Sun in Strength

The countenance of the sun represents the apostle's responsibility to reflect Christ in his ministry. As the apostle executes his ministry, Jesus' image and brightness should always be seen and not the glory of the apostle.

> *But God forbid that I should glory, save in the cross of our Lord Jesus Christ, by whom the world is crucified unto me, and I unto the world. (Galatians 6:14)*

God humbles the apostle, produces love in the apostle, and builds him in Christ's image so that the apostle has the proper conduct and character in ministry.

The Apostle's Character: *Fruit of the Spirit*

The apostle's ministry is not only based upon what they do (which is subjective to the will of God), but also in who they are. Mature apostles are known primarily by their godly characters and secondarily by their ministries. Before exploring the functions of the apostle in detail, the apostle's character has to be addressed.

> *But the fruit of the Spirit is love, joy, peace, longsuffering, gentleness, goodness, faith, meekness, temperance: against such there is no law. (Galatians 5:22-23)*

The apostle's character finds it definition within the person of Christ. To represent Christ fully, the apostle's character has to mirror the fruit of the Spirit. The fruit of the Spirit must then become the "fruit of the apostolic character."

Love

Love has to be the foundation of the apostle's ministry. God is love. Christ demonstrated His love for us through His obedience to God and His death on the cross. God's involvement with men is always through His love. His correction and discipline is rooted in love. The apostle has to be the express image of God. No matter what his ministry entails, it must be done through love.

> ***Charity suffereth long, and is kind; charity envieth not; charity vaunteth not itself, is not puffed up, doth not behave itself unseemly, seeketh not her own, is not easily provoked, thinketh no evil; rejoiceth not in iniquity, but rejoiceth in the truth; Beareth all things, believeth all things, hopeth all things, endureth all things. (I Corinthians 13:4-7)***

The apostle has to have an everlasting love for God, the Church, and his family. If he rebukes, corrects, admonishes, teaches, warns, and prays, love has to be the source. The apostle's demonstration of love must match Paul's description of love as recorded in I Corinthians 13.

Joy

Apostles are carriers of the good news. Though they are driven men, they should also be men of joy. While writing to the Romans, Paul dealt with strife between believers over non-doctrinal issues. At the end of his discourse, he said these words,

> ***For the kingdom of God is not eating and drinking, but righteousness, JOY, and peace in the Holy Spirit. (Romans14:17 NASV Emphasis mine)***

The apostles possess the message of the kingdom. Part of that message is joy. They must teach believers how to remain joyful in the midst of adverse situations.

Peace

Apostles must be ministers of peace. Apostolic ministry puts them in the middle of conflict, but it must not be the result of the apostles' own personality traits. Apostles have to be led by peace and inspire peace in their audiences. Jesus prayed that we would have peace, though the gospel sets us against the world.

> **Peace I leave with you, my peace I give unto you: not as the world giveth, give I unto you. Let not your heart be troubled, neither let it be afraid. (John 14:27)**

Apostles, as senior representatives of Christ, must continue to remind the saints of the peace that He left for them. In addition, apostles must not be angry, bitter, or harsh, but governed by peace.

Patience

Patience is one of the hallmarks of true apostolic ministry. Apostles have to be men of patience as they minister to the Church. Patience is vital for this purpose-driven ministry. Apostles must have patience as they wait to see the fruits of their labors develop in the lives of believers. Paul spoke of this apostolic patience when he said,

> *I am become a fool in glorying; ye have compelled me: for I ought to have been commended of you: for in nothing am I behind the very chiefest apostles, though I be nothing. Truly the signs of an apostle were wrought among you in all patience, in signs, and wonders, and mighty deeds. For what is it wherein ye were inferior to other churches, except it be that I myself was not burdensome to you? Forgive me this wrong.*
> *(II Corinthians 12:11-13)*

Apostles are not to be "task masters" over the people of God. They must exercise patience as they execute their ministries.

Kindness

Apostles have to be kind. Because they exercise great authority in the Spirit, they have no excuse to be rude or mean. Some apostles use their ministries as an excuse for a lack of kindness.

> *For a bishop must be blameless, as the steward of God; not self-willed, not soon angry, not given to wine, no striker, not given to filthy lucre; But a lover of hospitality, a lover of good men, sober, just, holy, temperate.*
> *(Titus 1:7-8)*

37

Apostles have to know how to conduct themselves as recipients of the grace and mercy of God. With this understanding, their lives at home and among the saints must be in demonstration of the kindness of God.

Faithfulness

Every apostle must be faithful to the call of God. He must demonstrate loyalty to Christ and the Church. Apostles have to be unwavering in their commitment to God.

> **Let a man so account of us, as of the ministers of Christ, and stewards of the mysteries of God. Moreover, it is required in stewards, that a man be found faithful. (I Corinthians 4:1-2)**

Since apostolic ministry is confrontational, faithfulness will sustain the apostle in times of great adversity. One of God's attributes is faithfulness; therefore, the apostle has to be faithful as he carries out the will of God.

Gentleness

Apostles have to be gentle as they minister to the saints. They may have the right words, but the wrong delivery. In addition, they are to be gentle with family and friends. It is a required trait of the servant of the Lord.

And the servant of the Lord must not strive; but be gentle unto all men, apt to teach, patient, In meekness instructing those that oppose themselves; if God peradventure will give them repentance to the acknowledging of the truth. (II Timothy 2:24)

Self-Control

Apostles are to exercise self-control in every affair of their lives. Self-control is needed in the pulpit, on the mission field, or in their homes.

Not given to wine, no striker, not greedy of filthy lucre; but patient, not a brawler, not covetous; one that ruleth well his own house, having his children in subjection with all gravity. (I Timothy 3:3-4)

Anyone called to the apostolic ministry must remember that success in ministry is not in ministerial activities, but in the maintenance of character, integrity, and conduct. Godly character will determine the level of success of the apostles as they fulfill their functions in the Church.

4

The Office of the Apostle

We have examined what an apostle is, the call of an apostle, and the making of an apostle. At this time, we will explore the apostle's role in the Church. There is a diversity in the demonstration and expression of apostolic ministry. Apostolic ministry manifests itself in various ways. However, there is some common ground among all apostles. No matter what their specific call is, apostles will exhibit characteristics of ambassadors, fathers, and husbands as they minister in the Church.

Apostles as Ambassadors

Every apostle is unique in his ministry. However, the apostle's role in the kingdom of God may parallel an ambassador's role in any earthly kingdom. Ambassadors are important to any nation. Oftentimes, they carry the nation's peace, prosperity, and safety by their words and actions. Though every member of the Body of Christ functions as an

41

ambassador for Him at some time, it is the primary role of the apostle. Paul compared apostolic ministry to that of an ambassador.

> *So, we as Christ's ambassadors, God making His appeal as it were through us. We {as Christ's personal representative} beg you for His sake to lay hold of the divine power [now offered you] and be reconciled to God. (II Corinthians 5:20 Amplified)*

Ambassadors are the highest officials and/or representatives in government. The word translated ambassador in the New Testament comes from the Greek word "presbeuo." It means to be a senior representative. Therefore, we conclude that among those God call into ministry, the apostle is the senior representative of the kingdom of God.

God set the apostles in the Church first, so that they could function as the ambassadors of the kingdom of God to the world's kingdom. They above all the other ministers must represent the kingdom of God as if Christ were still in the earth.

Ambassadors are sent forth with specific guidelines of the one who sent them. An ambassador does not choose what his assignment is. The ruler or government decides this. An ambassador does not become or function as an ambassador unless designated. The same is true for the apostle. The Lord appoints an apostle.

Individuals cannot lay claim to this office because of gifts, talents, and the advice of men. Jesus chose the apostles. If someone feels called to this office, the Lord will make it clear. However, one must remember that every apostle has a specific call on his life. Though he has great authority, only God directs him as to how to administer it.

Ambassador's influence is limited to that given by ruler or government. An ambassador only has influence in the countries that his government gives him. For instance, an ambassador to China may not have the same influence in Japan, if not sanctioned by the sending government.

Apostles only have authority over what God gives them. An apostle over one organization cannot assume apostleship over any organization or people in the Kingdom of God. God, alone, gives him his sphere of influence. Some apostolic ministers have ignored this fact and tried to usurp authority in churches and organizations where the Lord has not sent them. The apostle only has authority and influence in the places where God has sent them.

Ambassador's words are equal to the one that sent them. When ambassadors are commissioned, they are to speak as the ruler or government. Wars have begun and ended because of decisions made by the ambassadors. Above all the other offices, the apostles are to represent the voice of Christ and be in his stead as they minister in the Church. Apostles are expected to speak and act even as Christ would. Apostles have to possess the nature of Christ. The apostle's actions have to be a reflection of the mind of Christ operating in them. (I Corinthians 2:16)

Ambassadors have an invested/inherent authority.
Ambassadors are sent out with all authority and power of the commissioning government. Since they stand in place of the governing leadership, they walk in their power. Ambassadors are given this authority that they may fulfill their commission. Ambassadors cannot assume authority that is not given to them.

Apostles also have an invested authority. Their authority does not come because of what they do or who they are. Apostles do not have authority because they are apostles, but because God gives it to them. Apostles have to resist the temptation to abuse the authority God gives them.

> *For though I should boast somewhat more of our authority, which the Lord hath given us for edification, and not for your destruction, I should not be ashamed. (II Corinthians 10:8)*

If apostles abuse their authority, it will result in the destruction of the Body of Christ. There are numerous accounts in the Church today of apostles who misuse their power.

Ambassadors are expected to have wisdom, counsel, and knowledge of their ruler. Ambassadors are entrusted with the responsibility of representing those who sent them. Therefore, the training and discipline placed upon them is great. They must have personal integrity and character. In addition, they must be able to represent those who have commissioned them with knowledge and dignity.

Apostles are no different. They, too, must possess the wisdom, knowledge, and personality of Christ. Because they walk in the very authority of Christ, the training and discipline of God is oftentimes grave. This is so that when they speak, they will speak as an oracle of God, even more so, they will speak in Christ's stead.

Apostles as Fathers

The role of an apostle in the Church is not only to be an ambassador for Christ, but also to serve as a "father" ministry. The apostle's role in the kingdom is similar to that of a father. The apostles, themselves, referred to themselves as fathers and to those who partook of their ministry as their children. While writing to the Corinthian church, Paul likened his ministry unto a father. John called the saints his children.

> *For if you were to have countless tutors in Christ, yet you would not have many fathers; for in Christ Jesus I became your father through the gospel. (I Corinthians 4:15 NASV)*

45

My little children, these things write I unto you, that ye sin not. And if any man sin, we have an advocate with the Father, Jesus Christ the righteous. (I John 2:1)

The apostle will love the Church as a father loves his children. His personality in the Church will resemble that of a father.

Fathers provide for their children. As an earthly father provides for the needs of his children, the apostle will supply the spiritual needs of those entrusted to him. He will endeavor to ensure that the Church has the right information to live in this world in victory. They will strive to lay proper foundations in the lives of the people of God; that they may inherit the kingdom of God. Paul wrote,

Behold, the third time I am ready to come to you; and I will not be burdensome to you: for I seek not yours, but you: for the children ought not to lay up for the parents, but the parents for the children. And I will very gladly spend and be spent for you; though the more abundantly I love you, the less I be loved. (II Corinthians 12:14-15)

He explained to those at Corinth that as a father works and provides (spends) for his children, so he labors and expends his time, energy, and effort to provide for them spiritually. He wanted their souls to be saved.

Apostles have to avoid becoming "lord" and "kings" over the people of God. God has set them in the Church to serve.

Fathers nurture their children. Though a father provides for his children, provision without nurture handicaps a child. An apostle must not only labor in the Church, his labor has to be goal oriented. Whatever the apostle's specific call is, his concern will be a personal one.

> *But I (Paul and other apostles) proved to be gentle among you, as a nursing mother tenderly cares for her own children. (I Thessalonians 2:7 NASV, Parenthesis mine)*

The apostle's personal concern has to be tempered with grace and patience. Because God uses them to bring order and stability, some apostles become harsh in their words and demeanor. The anointing of God is not to be blamed for character flaws.

Fathers discipline their children. If a child has no discipline or training, he is liable to develop into a corrupt adult. The same is true for believers. If Christians are not disciplined, they will not grow up into mature saints.

Apostles will execute judgment and discipline in the Church. However, love is to be the motivation for the rebuke. John demonstrated this apostolic authority in his third epistle.

47

For this reason, if I come, I will call attention to his deeds which he does, unjustly accusing us with the wicked words; and not satisfied with this, neither does he himself receive the brethren, and he forbid those who desire to do so, and puts them out of the Church. (3 John verse 10 NASV)

John says that he will "call attention" to what a divisive minister did. He was expressing that he would personally deal with the individual because of his error.

Paul, on numerous occasions, exercised judgment and meted out discipline in the Church. While away from Corinth, news reached him that a brother was sleeping with this stepmother. He not only rebuked the church for not handling the situation, but also gave instruction concerning the discipline of the brother.

It is reported commonly that there is fornication among you, and such fornication as is not so much as named among the Gentiles, that one should have his father's wife. And ye are puffed up, and have not rather mourned, that he that hath done this deed might be taken away from among you. For I verily, as absent in body, but present in spirit, have judged already, as though I were present, concerning him that hath so done this deed, In the name of our Lord Jesus Christ,

> *when ye are gathered together, and my spirit,*
> *with the power of our Lord Jesus Christ, To*
> *deliver such an one unto Satan for the*
> *destruction of the flesh, that the spirit may be*
> *saved in the day of the Lord Jesus. (I*
> *Corinthians 5:1-5)*

Paul meted out discipline. However, it was for the salvation of the offender. True fathers discipline their children to save them. When the apostle rebukes, it has to be done in love, else he will offend one of God's very own. He must remember that he has a Father in heaven.

Fathers give wise/sound instruction to their children. The book of Proverbs is a compilation of instructions that a father would give to his children. Fathers seek to instill knowledge in their children. A father will pass on the information that he has learned. Apostles will impart revelation and knowledge to the Church as a father does to his children.

> *And they continued stedfastly in the apostles'*
> *doctrine and fellowship, and in breaking of*
> *bread, and in prayers. (Acts 2:42)*

> *But, beloved, remember ye the words which*
> *were spoken before of the apostles of our Lord*
> *Jesus Christ. (Jude verse17)*

The Church was established on the apostle's teaching. Peter instructed them to remember what had been previously taught. He did not cite the teaching of other elders and leaders, but what the apostles taught.

Apostles are expected to give fatherly wisdom and instruction in the Church.

Nine Functions of the Apostle

Though there are varieties of ministries and operations, apostles have essentially the same functions. Some functions are not exclusive to apostles. However, apostles will differ from other ministries in the execution of those functions.

Preach & Teach the Word of God (I Tim. 2:7). Apostles are gifted to preach and/or teach the word of God under divine inspiration and authority. They are anointed to make known the mysteries of God through the Word. This is performed with boldness and sobriety.

> *Let a man so account of us (apostles), as of the ministers of Christ, and stewards of the mysteries of God. (I Corinthians 4:1 Parenthesis mine)*

Impart Spiritual Gifts (Acts 8:17; Romans 1:11; II Tim. 1:6). Apostles have the ability to bring forth the gifts of God in believers. They have the power to impart wisdom, knowledge, and understanding. Apostles can bring to light the spiritual gifts resident in believers and impart gifts (by revelation of the Spirit) through the laying on of hands.

> *Neglect not the gift that is in thee, which was*

given thee by prophecy, with the laying on of the hands of the presbytery. (I Timothy 4:14)

Establish and/or Oversee Churches and Organizations. Because apostles are sent with a divine message, God uses some to start organizations as vehicles to present their messages. In addition, apostles will start new churches and ministries in areas where they are sent to preach. This is to give structure to those who have heard the message. For example, Paul and Barnabas started many churches to give the new converts some organization to the worship of God.

> *And some days after Paul said unto Barnabas, Let us go again and visit our brethren in every city where we have preached the word of the Lord, and see how they do. (Acts 15:36)*

Evangelize. Every apostle has a message. Apostles are gifted to go into areas that have not been open to the gospel or areas that are stagnant. Jesus sent the original twelve out to preach. Every apostle will function as an evangelist, whether to the Church (to bring balance and order) or to the Lost (for redemption and salvation).

> *For so hath the Lord commanded us, saying, I have set thee to be a light of the Gentiles, that thou shouldest be for salvation unto the ends of the earth. And when the Gentiles heard this, they were glad, and glorified the word of the*

Lord: and as many as were ordained to eternal life believed. And the word of the Lord was published throughout all the region. (Acts 13:47-49)

Raise Up Leaders (Acts 15:39; II Tim. 2:1-2; Acts 6:3-6). Because of the authority given to them, apostles have the anointing and responsibility to raise up leaders. This is done for the advancement of the kingdom of God.

Apostles will have "Timothys" and "Elishas" in ministry so that the work of the Lord will continue after they have left the scene. If an apostle is the head of a religious organization, he will have the ability to recognize gifts and ministries in individuals and set them in the Church as directed by the Spirit.

To Titus, mine own son after the common faith: Grace, mercy, and peace, from God the Father and the Lord Jesus Christ our Saviour. For this cause left I thee in Crete, that thou shouldest set in order the things that are wanting, and ordain elders in every city, as I had appointed thee. (Titus 1:4-5)

Expose False Apostles & Doctrine. Apostles are stewards of over the mysteries of God. They have the wisdom and foresight to warn against deception. They will contend for purity of faith and doctrine in the Church. They, like the prophets of old, will warn and speak against false apostles openly.

> *But there were false prophets also among the*
> *people, even as there shall be false teachers*
> *among you, who privily shall bring in*
> *damnable heresies, even denying the Lord that*
> *bought them, and bring upon themselves swift*
> *destruction. And many shall follow their*
> *pernicious ways; by reason of whom the way*
> *of truth shall be evil spoken of. (II Peter 2:1-2)*

Perform Signs, Wonders, Healings, & Miracles. The apostle has a miraculous ministry. Apostles are gifted men, not only to perform signs and wonders, but in the revelation gifts of the Spirit. The word of knowledge, word of wisdom, discerning of spirits, and prophecy will operate regularly in their ministries.

> *And fear came upon every soul; and many*
> *wonders and signs were done by the apostles.*
> *(Acts 2:43)*

Lay Spiritual Foundations in the Church. Apostles have the authority and anointing to lay spiritual foundations in the Church. Though no modern-day apostles will write scripture, they are equipped to reveal the hidden truths of God's Word and lay the proper foundation for the people of God to grow thereby.

> *Whereby, when ye read, ye may understand my*
> *knowledge in the mystery of Christ) which in*
> *other ages was not made known unto the sons*
> *of men, as it is now revealed unto his holy*

apostles and prophets by the Spirit. (Ephesians 3:4-5)

Establish Churches in the Faith (Gospel). Apostles have the unique ability to bring people back to the purity of the faith. They are able to instruct babes in Christ until they become mature in their personal relationships with God and in their doctrinal beliefs. They can promote stability and growth in the Body of Christ.

> *And as they went through the cities, they delivered them the decrees for to keep, that were ordained of the apostles and elders which were at Jerusalem. And so were the churches established in the faith, and increased in number daily. (Acts 16:4-5)*

Though there are many dimensions to this awesome ministry (not listed), most apostles will demonstrate all of these functions at some time in their ministries.

Focus of Apostles

The focus and thrust of apostles is reflective of the role of the heart in the human body. The heart is the central location for where blood is pumped to the rest of the body. It is said to house our innermost feelings and emotions. Apostles endeavor to reveal to the Church the heart of God. They have a love for God and strive to make others aware of the love of God towards them.

54

Apostles strive to see the Church advance in the Kingdom of God. In the same manner that the heart pumps blood throughout the Body, they will make sure believers walk in the newness of life by their continual ministering in the Church. Though apostles have a zeal for order and structure in the Church, it must be balanced by love.

Apostolic individuals will know how to express the innermost heart of God and bring people into a father-child relationship with the Lord. At the core, apostles want to see men and women be conformed to the likeness and image of Christ. The heart of God from the beginning was to have sons and daughters. The apostolic ministry is given to see this fulfilled in this life.

5

The Apostolic Person

We have learned that the apostolic ministry was displayed first in the New Testament Church. Its role in the Church has been influential from the beginning. However, not everyone in the Church is an apostle. There is diversity in the Body of Christ.

> *Now ye are the body of Christ, and members in particular. And God hath set some in the church, first apostles, secondarily prophets, thirdly teachers, after that miracles, then gifts of healings, helps, governments, diversities of tongues. Are all apostles? Are all prophets? Are all teachers? Are all workers of miracles? Have all the gifts of healing? Do all speak with tongues? Do all interpret? (I Corinthians 12:27-31)*

Since our body has many parts, so does the Body of Christ. Paul explained that the Church was the same as a physical body. He taught that the Body of Christ was made up of many members and that each had a particular function. He concluded this portion of his argument by showing how God developed offices and gifts in the Church beginning with the apostles.

Afterwards, to further illustrate his point of diversity, he asks a series of questions to which the answer is a resounding "NO!" All are not apostles and all or not prophets, and so on.

Since all are not apostles, God makes the benefit of apostolic ministry available to all by placing an apostolic anointing on other members in the Body. The individual who possesses an apostolic anointing is referred to as an apostolic person. The apostolic person has a passion for Christ and the Church and an unwavering faith in God.

The apostolic anointing is as broad as the apostolic office. However, there are certain characteristics that apostolic individuals share. No matter what their individual functions are in the Church, apostolic people will exhibit the characteristics of disciples, sons, and big brothers.

The Apostolic Person is a Disciple

Apostolic people have a consuming passion and desire for Christ. They follow Christ daily. As the disciples left all to serve Christ, they will leave the world behind to please Him.

Disciples are students and pupils. Apostolic people have a hunger and love for the things of God. They have a passion not only to learn of Him, but also to become as He is. The Word of God has priority in their lives.

Disciples follow their masters whole-heartedly. Apostolic people will follow Christ with all of their hearts. They have the ability to endure every trial and test in order to follow Him.

Disciples are disciplined. Apostolic people will have a zeal for the holiness of God. Their lives will reflect the necessary discipline and self-control needed to remain in right standing with the Lord.

Disciples have one goal: to become like their instructors. Apostolic people have a desire to be like Christ. Their goal is to reflect His image in their everyday lives. They have an undying urge to bring honor and glory to the Master.

Disciples respect their instructors. Apostolic people have respect for Christ and His representatives. They will respect leadership in the Church and in the government.

The Apostolic Person is a Son (or Daughter)

Apostolic people believe that God wants relationship above religion and sonship above service. They strive to be sons (and daughters) of God.

Sons are obedient to their parents. Apostolic people will be true sons and daughters in ministry. Even as Timothy was a son unto Paul, they will exemplify this in their relationships with Church leadership. Not only will they be subject to leadership, but more importantly to the Word of God and the leading of His Spirit.

Sons reflect the image of their fathers. Apostolic people endeavor to reflect the nature and character of Christ. They will be godly individuals reflecting the holiness of God. They follow the verse of scripture that states, "Be ye holy; for I am holy." (I Peter 1:16)

Sons follow the father's examples. Apostolic people believe that whatsoever things they have seen Christ do, they can do also. They will not only demonstrate the character and nature of God, but His works will follow them. They do not need a position or title, they believe because He said so. Apostolic believe unquestionably in the following scriptures,

> *And these signs shall follow them that believe; In my name shall they cast out devils; they shall speak with new tongues; They shall take up serpents; and if they drink any deadly thing, it shall not hurt them; they shall lay hands on the sick, and they shall recover. (Mark 16:17-18)*

> *Verily, verily, I say unto you, He that believeth on me, the works that I do shall he do also; and greater works than these shall he do; because I go unto my Father. (I John 14:12)*

The Apostolic Person is a Brother (or Sister)

The apostolic person believes in the family of the Church. They relate to other believers as if they were biological brothers and sisters. Their concern is genuine and heart-felt.

Big brothers protect their siblings. Apostolic people are watchful over their brothers and sisters in Christ. They will help immature and weak Christians in their walks. They believe that they are their brother's keeper. They will be sensitive to the needs of others through the Spirit of God.

Big brothers enforce their parent's rules to their siblings. Apostolic people respect God and Church leadership. They will remind their brothers and sisters to follow the Word, the Spirit, and their leaders. They will endeavor to see others walk in obedience to Christ and leadership.

Big brothers earn the trust of their parents. Apostolic people are respected by the leaders they serve under and by fellow believers. Leaders will trust their advice and council because they do not seek to please themselves, but to please God and to serve leadership faithfully. Apostolic people will also have the respect of other members in the Body of Christ. This is due to the love and respect that they demonstrate towards Christ, leadership, and the brethren.

The Apostolic Person's Character

Because the apostolic person has the favor of God, the respect of leadership, and the support of the brethren, they must strive to reflect the nature of Christ at all times and resist pride. Paul gives the necessary character traits of apostolic people in his instructions to the Roman Church (Romans 12:9-17)

1. Apostolic people have to demonstrate genuine love. They must be lovers of good and despisers of evil in all forms. (Romans 12:9)

2) Apostolic people must love the brethren and seek the welfare of others above themselves. (Romans 12:10)

3) Apostolic people have to resist procrastination and stagnation in ministry. They must maintain a zeal for the work of the Lord. (Romans 12:11)

4) Apostolic people have to be people of faith and prayer. They have to be able to endure tribulation, inspire hope in others and themselves, and be prayer warriors. (Romans 12:12)

5) Apostolic people have to be selfless. They must be willing to meet the needs of others and to be easily entreated. (Romans 12:13)

6) Apostolic people should speak words that edify and build up other believers at all times. They are not to be gossips and revilers. (Romans 12:14)

7) Apostolic people have to be in tune with other members of the Body. They, through the Spirit, have to be sensitive to the failures, trials, and successes of others. (Romans 12:15)

8) Apostolic people have to be impartial in their relationships with others. They should be as God who is no respecter of persons. (Romans 12:16)

62

9) Apostolic people have to be harmless. They ought to be gentle, representing the nature of God in all honesty. (Romans 12:17)

Anyone who feels he/she has an apostolic anointing has to guard themselves against pride, deception, and visions of greatness. In turn, they will be pillars in the midst of the Church.

Recognizing the Apostolic Person

The apostolic person will function uniquely in the Body of Christ. In order to recognize the apostolic person, one has to know the functions of apostolic individuals.

Apostolic people carry the Word of God. Apostolic people understand and know how to make proper application of the scriptures. They, like apostles, will understand many of the hidden things of God through scripture. They encourage other believers to study the Word of God.

> *Study to shew thyself approved unto God, a workman that needeth not to be ashamed, rightly dividing the word of truth. But shun profane and vain babblings: for they will increase unto more ungodliness. (II Timothy 2:15)*

Apostolic people impart life into other believers. Apostolic people know how to communicate spiritual truths to help other believers grow in the knowledge of

63

the Lord. Their words will consistently minister grace, wisdom, insight, hope, and faith to those around them.

> *Let no corrupt communication proceed out of your mouth, but that which is good to the use of edifying, that it may minister grace unto the hearers. (Ephesians 4:29)*

Apostolic people help establish others in their walks with the Lord. Apostolic people have the spiritual insight to help babes and immature saints gain strength in the Lord. They will help them to overcome weaknesses and sins through wise counsel, prayer, and support.

> *Brethren, if a man be overtaken in a fault, ye which are spiritual, restore such an one in the spirit of meekness; considering thyself, lest thou also be tempted. Bear ye one another's burdens, and so fulfill the law of Christ. (Galatians 6:1-2)*

Apostolic people are shameless witnesses of the Lord. Apostolic people are gifted to evangelize in the name of the Lord. Whether at home, at work, or out in public, they seek to win souls to the Kingdom of God. They realize that their relationship with God, not a title, compels them to witness. They do this with great conviction and results.

> *But ye shall receive power, after that the Holy Ghost is come upon you: and ye shall be witnesses unto me both in Jerusalem, and in all Judaea, and in Samaria, and unto the uttermost part of the earth. (Acts 1:8)*

Apostolic people serve and support leadership. Apostolic people believe in divine order. They will support godly leadership without question. No matter what capacity they serve in the Church, it is done as unto the Lord and with respect unto God-given leadership. They also encourage others to follow the leadership as they follow the Lord.

> *Remember them which have the rule over you, who have spoken unto you the word of God: whose faith follow, considering the end of their conversation. (Hebrews 13:17)*

Apostolic people expose false doctrines and ministers. Apostolic people exercise mature discernment. They are zealous for the Lord and the purity of the Church. They have the wisdom to recognize false ministers and doctrines readily. They are bold in identifying the false while supporting the truth.

> *Beware of false prophets, which come to you in sheep's clothing, but inwardly they are ravening wolves. Ye shall know them by their fruits. Do men gather grapes of thorns, or figs of thistles? (Matthew 7:15-16)*

Apostolic people possess the power and gifts of the Spirit. Apostolic people have the gifts in operation in their lives. They believe God in all things. They are believers who have powerful testimonies of the power of God being displayed in their everyday lives.

> *And these signs shall follow them that believe; In my name shall they cast out devils; they*

shall speak with new tongues; They shall take up serpents; and if they drink any deadly thing, it shall not hurt them; they shall lay hands on the sick, and they shall recover. (Mark 16:17-18)

Though apostolic people are scattered through out the Body of Christ, no matter where they are they bring life and stability among the congregation.

Flowing as an Apostolic Person

If you believe there is an apostolic anointing upon your life, there are certain practical steps to take to flow properly in it. Without these disciplines in your life, you will never flow fully in what God has for you.

Study the Word of God. Apostolic people have to consistently study and apply the Word of God to their lives. The Word has to rule their hearts and minds. The Word will equip them for service in the Body of Christ. Apostolic people have to believe the scriptures are trustworthy. They must have faith that the Word is directly from God.

All scripture is given by inspiration of God, and is profitable for doctrine, for reproof, for correction, for instruction in righteousness: That the man of God may be perfect, thoroughly furnished unto all good works. (II Timothy 3:16-17)

Have an established prayer life. Apostolic people have to be consistent in prayer. It is the only way to

66

remain strong in the Lord. In addition, prayer will give them greater sensitivity in the Spirit. Prayer will guide them to their rightful places in ministry. They should have a heart to pray also for local leadership that nothing hinders the spreading of the gospel.

> *Praying always with all prayer and supplication in the Spirit, and watching thereunto with all perseverance and supplication for all saints. (Ephesians 6:18)*

Follow Leadership. Apostolic people have to be submitted to local leadership. They must follow the vision of the leaders as they follow Christ. Without being submitted to authority, they will become ineffective in the Church.

> *Remember them which have the rule over you, who have spoken unto you the word of God: whose faith follow, considering the end of their conversation. (Hebrews 13:7)*

Understanding of the apostolic office and anointing is useless unless we develop a proper perspective for this ministry. In the next chapter, we will discuss the proper perspective the Church is to have towards the apostolic ministry.

6

Apostles in Perspective

The increase of revelation and information opens up the path to deception through excess. As we endeavor to learn more about God and His ministries, we must avoid extremes. History has shown that every time God has moved in the earth, the enemy has tried to counter attack with excess and deception. We see this trend today with the emerging apostolic ministries.

In this chapter, we will endeavor to bring balance to the numerous teachings surrounding apostles. In short, we want to keep our outlook on the office in perspective.

Apostles and the Church

In the first chapter, we stated that apostolic ministry is a foundational ministry in the Church. Foundational does not mean that this ministry is more important or valuable than other ministries. When considering a building, the foundation is not seen.

However, when storms and other influences come against the building, the foundation's strength provides support for the building.

The same is true for the Church. When apostles minister properly, they will not be the center of attention, but the entire Church will display the nature of Christ and the power of God.

The true purpose of apostles is that their ministries help the Church stand against attacks of the enemy and deception. However, we see that the Church has lost vision, purpose, and power. This is because true apostolic ministry is missing. Consequently, the Church promotes false doctrines and ministers unwittingly. In addition, it is divided over unimportant issues. The Church has left the simplicity of Christ to follow another gospel, based upon prosperity and not righteousness.

> *But I fear, lest by any means, as the serpent beguiled Eve through his subtilty, so your minds should be corrupted from the simplicity that is in Christ. For if he that cometh preacheth another Jesus, whom we have not preached, or if ye receive another spirit, which ye have not received, or another gospel, which ye have not accepted, ye might well bear with him. (II Corinthians 11:3-4)*

The error of many apostles is that they have drawn attention to themselves and their gifts and have neglected their responsibilities to the Church. As a result, the whole Church suffers. Apostles are to minister so that the Church may shine.

> *For all things are for your sakes, that the abundant grace might through the thanksgiving of many redound to the glory of God. (II Corinthians 4:15)*

> *Therefore I endure all things for the elect's sakes, that they may also obtain the salvation which is in Christ Jesus with eternal glory. (II Timothy 2:10)*

Modern day apostles are to have this mentality as they minister. They minister so the Church would remain partakers of the grace of God unto salvation. The foundation supports the building. When apostles fulfill their tasks, local assemblies, churches, and organizations are healthy and vibrant.

The problem remains that individuals in the Body of Christ are exalting apostles, prophets, and other ministers above measure in the Church. The Church has to be sober in its acceptance of apostles. They have to remember that apostles are individuals redeemed by Christ. Their gifts do not make them special or superior.

Their gifts and ministries make them responsible for the Church. Many apostles fall into pride and rebellion because men esteem them too highly. What, then, is to be the Church's approach to apostles?

> *For I say, through the grace given unto me, to every man that is among you, not to think of himself more highly than he ought to think; but to think soberly, according as God hath dealt to every man the measure of faith. For as we have many members in one body, and all members have not the same office: So we, being many, are one body in Christ, and every one members one of another. (Romans 12:3-5)*

Paul instructed the Romans that they were not to think too much of themselves. However, we must remember not to think too much of apostles. Why? He goes on to say that God has given every man a measure of faith to operate in whatever ministry or gift he has. Therefore, since God is the source of all gifts, there is no need for the saints to think of anyone too highly. Yet, we are to give respect and honor unto one another as members of Christ.

> *Render therefore to all their dues: tribute to whom tribute is due; custom to whom custom; fear to whom fear; honour to whom honour. (Romans 13:7)*

Paul told the Romans that they were to give respect unto the leaders in government. Whatever office they held, he told them to give them the respect the office demanded. The same applies to apostles, prophets, and other ministries. We are to respect them for their service in the Lord, especially those who labor for our spiritual well-being (this speaks very heavily to pastors).

> *For if a man think himself to be something, when he is nothing, he deceiveth himself. But let every man prove his own work, and then shall he have rejoicing in himself alone, and not in another. (Galatians 6:3-4)*

Apostles are not to boast about their labors, for it leads to deception. Conversely, they are to rejoice before the Lord because of the reward He gives.

Apostles and Pastors

The enemy is the author of confusion and division. If he can keep the leaders in the Church divided, they will not minister effectively in the Church. We have already addressed the fact that apostles are not to think more highly of themselves than they ought. However, since pastors usually have the oversight of local churches and assemblies, there is a need for understanding between apostles and pastors.

At the heart of the strife and tension between apostles and pastors is the need for control blurred by personal insecurities. When a pastor has an apostle in his church, he must not allow insecurity and intimidation to grip his spirit. If so, he will perceive everything the apostle does as a challenge to his authority.

73

Conversely, the apostle should not try to handle situations reserved for the pastor of the Church. The pastor has the responsibility for the souls of the sheep. He also bears the responsibility for the spiritual oversight of the apostles that are in fellowship with the assembly.

Oftentimes, the enemy causes a war between pastors and apostles. The pastors feel intimidated by the manner in which God uses the apostles, and the apostles feel that the pastor is against them because of a persecution complex. The need for communication is vital.

Without communication, there will be confusion and no one will benefit, but the kingdom of Satan. Pastors have to resist fighting apostles to feel like they are in control. Control is not the issue, but ministry. However, apostles have to learn to be subject to leadership if they expect to have fruitful ministries.

All ministries are needed in the Body of Christ. Pastors cannot devalue the ministries of apostles because they are under their ministries. Pastors need to understand that this ministry is foundational and is an asset to any ministry.

Conversely, prophets cannot feel that they are "above" pastors because of the authority and anointing upon their lives. Ministries are given to work together in peace. It is with this understanding that apostles and

74

pastors have to work together in the local church or assembly.

Apostles versus Prophets

Another reoccurring trend in the Body of Christ is apostles trying to function as prophets and prophets trying to function as apostles without the anointing or call of the Lord. Apostles will have to function sometimes in prophetic voices in the Body of Christ. However, this is not to be their area of concern. Their main job is to advance the Kingdom of God, not to be prophets.

Because some apostles have become deceived, thinking that they are all of the ministry gifts wrapped into one, they began to prophesy beyond the measure of their gifts. This turns into a soulish prophetic ministry, which usually ends up with the apostle thinking that he cannot ever be wrong.

The apostle then begins to prophesy for money and personal gain. Then, the apostle usually develops a following based upon his personality rather than the person of Christ. The result is then a deceived apostle with a following of beguiled souls.

Prophets also have to guard themselves against thinking that God is going to elevate them to the apostolic office. It is true that Paul was a prophet/teacher before entering into apostolic ministry. However, this was at the call of the *Lord*. With some,

75

God does use the prophetic office as training for the apostolic office.

Many prophets, though, have taken it upon *themselves* to try to operate as apostles. They begin to start ministries and churches claiming apostolic authority and right. The result is a deceived prophet whose prophetic ministry is stifled by deception.

Though there are similarities between apostles and prophets, they must resist intruding on one another's offices based upon their own desires. In addition, apostles and prophets have to resist competing among themselves as to which office takes preeminence in the Church.

The Word declares that He placed the apostles first. However, all ministries are equally important to the plan and purpose of God in the earth. No ministry is better, though functions differ.

Apostles and prophets have to learn how to relate to one another through the Spirit, balanced by humility and love. In order for the church to keep Apostles and Apostolic ministry in the proper perspective, misconceptions of this office have to be addressed.

Misconceptions

There are many false beliefs circulating about apostles and their ministries. We shall now explore some of the prevailing misconceptions surrounding the apostolic office.

I. Paul is not the standard for all apostles.

One mistake that Christian theologians have made is to make the ministry of Paul the standard for all apostles. Scholars infer that Paul is the barometer for all apostles because his ministry is highlighted more than others. However, God operates in diversity even among those with the same ministry. Though Peter and Paul were apostles, Galatians informs us that they did not minister to the same group, or in the same manner.

> *On the contrary, they saw that I had been entrusted with the task of preaching the gospel to the Gentiles, just as Peter had been to the Jews. For God, who was at work in the ministry of Peter as an apostle to the Jews, was also at work in my ministry as an apostle to the Gentiles. (Galatians 2:7-8 NIV)*

II. Not all apostles will do evangelistic work, though they will be involved.

In the scriptures, we read of apostles like Peter, Paul, Barnabas, and Apollos who traveled frequently and ministered. However, other apostles were stationary like James and the other apostles located in Jerusalem. The scriptures give no indication that these men traveled extensively, but numerous accounts are given of these men sending emissaries to monitor the growth of the Church. Among those sent from them were Paul, Barnabas, Judas and Silas, Agabus and other prophets, and Peter.

> *Then pleased it the apostles and elders, with the whole church, to send chosen men of their own company to Antioch with Paul and Barnabas; namely, Judas surnamed Barsabas, and Silas, chief men among the brethren. (Acts 15:22)*

III. Not all apostles will start churches.

Because of the ministry of Paul and Barnabas, it has become the rule that apostles will start churches. James, who exercised oversight in Jerusalem, did not start the work there. Paul and Barnabas had to start churches in order to give the Gentiles an order for the worship of God. They went in areas where Christ was not preached. Therefore, they had to start churches and appoint leaders. Please remember, a sign of the apostolic anointing is the starting of churches and organizations, but it is not mandatory.

The scriptures give no indication that this is a qualification to be an apostle. If we hold to this belief, we would have to call every leader that has started a church, organization, or ministry, an apostle. We know that this is not true. The qualification for apostolic ministry is based upon godly attributes and power.

Truly the signs of an apostle were wrought among you in all patience, in signs, and wonders, and mighty deeds. (II Corinthians 12:12)

IV. An apostle is not an apostle over all.

Some immature apostles and leaders have promoted the doctrine that if someone is an apostle; they exercise apostolic authority over any church they choose. This is not true. An apostle is only an apostle where he is received as an apostle.

Yea, so have I strived to preach the gospel, not where Christ was named, lest I should build upon another man's foundation. (Romans 15:20)

Am I not an apostle? am I not free? have I not seen Jesus Christ our Lord? Are not ye my work in the Lord? If I be not an apostle unto others, yet doubtless I am to you: for the seal of mine apostleship are ye in the Lord. (I Corinthians 9:1-2)

Paul did not preach the gospel where any others had preached Christ, and he only exercised apostolic oversight over churches he established. He was given apostolic oversight over churches he did not start, at their request.

For I would that ye knew what great conflict I have for you, and for them at Laodicea, and for as many as have not seen my face in the flesh; That their hearts might be comforted, being knit together in love, and unto all riches of the full assurance of understanding, to the acknowledgement of the mystery of God, and of the Father, and of Christ. (Colossians 2:1-2)

V. Local churches do not need to be under an apostle's ministry.

It is true that any church that receives an apostle or is under a true apostle's ministry will be greatly blessed. However, there were numerous churches in the apostle's day that was not under apostolic control. The church at Antioch was started after the saints fled persecution (Acts 11:19). The elders at Jerusalem sent Paul and Barnabas to check on the work, not to take control.

The Jerusalem apostles and elders did not replace the leadership with their own elders. They left the church in the hands of those who began it. In addition, we find that at the church of Antioch, no apostles were named. Only prophets and teachers seemed to exercise rule and authority. We discover that these leaders were intricate in launching Paul and Barnabas into the apostolic ministry.

Now there were in the church that was at Antioch certain prophets and teachers; as Barnabas, and Simeon that was called Niger, and Lucius of Cyrene, and Manaen, which had been brought up with Herod the tetrarch, and Saul. As they ministered to the Lord, and fasted, the Holy Ghost said, Separate me Barnabas and Saul for the work whereunto I have called them. And when they had fasted and prayed, and laid their hands on them, they sent them away. (Acts 13:1-3)

VI. An apostle does not have to function in another ministry before operating in apostolic ministry.

With the acceptance of apostles came this restriction: To operate in apostolic ministry, one must first operate in another one of the ministry offices. It is true that some apostles operated in other ministries before they became apostles, this was the case with Paul and Barnabas.

In Antioch, Paul (Saul) and Barnabas were listed among the prophets and teachers. There are apostles, today, who have operated for years as prophets, evangelists, and pastors before God released them into the greater work. God used the other offices as their training. It will enhance the apostolic ministry in them.

If someone can teach, evangelize, pastor, and be a prophet without operating in another ministry, the

81

same holds true for the apostle. We read of men like James, Jude, and Apollos who were of note among the apostles without having operated in another capacity in the Church. Timothy and Titus were under Paul's instruction and then they were released into apostolic ministry to the churches where he sent them.

VII. Apostles are not exempt from accountability and Church authority. (I Timothy 5:20)

Apostles are not to be their own bosses. If they are heads of organizations, then they need to be in fellowship and accountability with other leaders. Also, if an apostle is not the overseer over a church, but has ministry; he must be in fellowship with a local assembly or governing body as any other saint. Apostles are not above rebuke, correction, and discipline. Paul rebuked Peter when he was in error.

> *But when Peter was come to Antioch, I withstood him to the face, because he was to be blamed. For before that certain came from James, he did eat with the Gentiles: but when they were come, he withdrew and separated himself, fearing them which were of the circumcision. And the other Jews dissembled likewise with him; insomuch that Barnabas also was carried away with their dissimulation. But when I saw that they walked not uprightly according to the truth of the gospel, I said unto Peter before them all, If thou, being a Jew, livest after the manner of Gentiles, and*

> *not as do the Jews, why compellest thou the Gentiles to live as do the Jews? (Galatians 2:11-14)*

If someone is an apostle, and the pastor is not, the apostolic minister is not above the local leader. The pastor is his head and he must be submitted to him. Paul submitted his ministry to the leadership in Jerusalem for counsel.

> *And I went up by revelation, and communicated unto them that gospel which I preach among the Gentiles, but privately to them which were of reputation, lest by any means I should run, or had run, in vain. (Galatians 2:2)*

Knowledge of the office the apostle is important to understanding the work of Christ in the Church. Illumination helps to develop an appreciation for this ministry and a desire to see it in operation along with the prophets, evangelists, pastors, and teachers.

7

What is Apostleship?

"I have an apostolic anointing." "I have been called as an apostle." "I am an apostle." These are expressions that are increasingly heard in the Body of Christ. Some believers are put off by them. Though some individuals who say this may be in error, God has placed the apostolic gift in the Body of Christ. It is not only reserved for those who are apostles, but for any believer whom the Spirit will endow.

The apostolic grace is a widely misunderstood gift; so, many are still confused about its use, function, and purpose. In this chapter, we want to discover the fulness of the apostolic gift and ministry in the Body of Christ. The totality of apostolic ministry is described in one word: *apostleship.* It is a term used by Paul to describe his ministry.

By whom we have received grace and apostleship, for obedience to the faith among all nations, for his name. (Romans 1:5)

85

However, apostleship is something that the Spirit will give to whom He will. The word *apostleship* means commission. There are individuals in the Body of Christ who are not apostles, but have a commission from God.

God operates in diversity. There are different aspects of apostleship demonstrated in the Body of Christ. There are levels to apostleship. As we discuss each, we will understand the purpose of apostleship in the Church.

The Apostolic Gift

In its simplest form, again, apostleship is a commission. There are individuals in the Body of Christ who have received a specific commission from the Lord. Individuals who receive such a commission share in the first level of apostleship. They have an apostolic gift.

The apostolic gift manifests in different ways. Ministers who have an apostolic gift will oftentimes start churches and religious organizations by the command of the Lord. They may not be apostles, but they will be sent to certain areas to pastor or start organizations whereby the Kingdom of God advances.

However, after the church is planted and the organization established, the apostolic gift takes a 'back seat' to the calling on their lives.

In the laity, individuals who have an apostolic gift will start departments and auxiliaries in their churches. They will have vision to see the local assembly grow. They will be faithful members in service.

Aside from organizational skills and abilities, anyone who has an apostolic gift will, at times, exercise authority in the Spirit. They will also demonstrate the power of God. They will be spiritually sensitive men and women who have only a desire to please Christ.

The Apostolic Anointing

There are individuals in the Church who are not apostles, but there is a definite apostolic touch on their lives and ministries. These individuals are said to possess an apostolic anointing. This is the next level of apostleship. How does this differ from someone who has an apostolic gift? In simple terms, the person who has an apostolic gift will demonstrate apostolic grace and ability occasionally.

However, an individual with an apostolic anointing will demonstrate apostolic power, grace, and authority regularly as they minister to the Body of Christ. Possessing an apostolic anointing does not place one in the office of the apostle, but it does make them a part of the emerging apostolic company of believers.

The apostolic anointing is seen oftentimes in believers who are called to the five-fold ministry. They will operate in their respective offices while exercising apostolic power and authority. The apostolic anointing adds a depth and dimension to their ministries. In addition, one does not have to be called to a ministry office to possess an apostolic anointing (discussed earlier). These individuals are strategically placed in the Body of Christ that all may be partakers of the apostolic ministry.

Individuals who possess an apostolic anointing will manifest the revelation and power of the Spirit consistently. They will have encounters with the Lord frequently. This may be in dreams and visions or in visitations of the Holy Spirit. In addition, they will be able to help others grow in their relationship with the Lord. Some will function like missionaries (sent ones) between churches. They will travel from assembly to assembly, strengthening pastors and leadership through their service.

The Apostolic Spirit

The greatest expression of apostleship is not in the apostolic gift, the apostolic anointing, or the ministry of the apostle. It is in the apostolic spirit. The early Church was effective because they appreciated and accepted the ministry of the apostles. As a result, great grace and power rested upon the thousands of believers in Jerusalem.

And they continued stedfastly in the apostles' doctrine and fellowship, and in breaking of bread, and in prayers. And fear came upon every soul: and many wonders and signs were done by the apostles. And all that believed were together, and had all things common; And sold their possessions and goods, and parted them to all men, as every man had need. And they, continuing daily with one accord in the temple, and breaking bread from house to house, did eat their meat with gladness and singleness of heart, Praising God, and having favour with all the people. And the Lord added to the church daily such as should be saved. (Acts 2:42-47)

The early Church demonstrated the apostolic spirit. This is the highest level of apostleship. Jesus' words to the apostles illustrate the manifestation of the apostolic spirit.

Go ye therefore, and teach all nations, baptizing them in the name of the Father, and of the Son, and of the Holy Ghost: Teaching them to observe all things whatsoever I have commanded you: and, lo, I am with you alway, even unto the end of the world. Amen. (Matthew 28:19-20)

In the Gospels, Jesus gives a charge to the apostles before He ascended. It is understood that the charge given to them is one that the Church is to fulfill corporately.

> *Go ye therefore, and teach all nations,*
> *baptizing them in the name of the Father, and*
> *of the Son, and of the Holy Ghost: Teaching*
> *them to observe all things whatsoever I have*
> *commanded you: and, lo, I am with you alway,*
> *even unto the end of the world. Amen.*
> *(Matthew 28:19-20)*

The Church is sent to the world to represent Christ.
The apostolic spirit represents the Church's
apostleship to the world. How does this affect the local
assembly? When an assembly embraces the apostolic
spirit, three things are evident. They are the same
things that were evident in the early Church.

1. **Unity** – When the apostolic spirit is manifested in
an assembly, every believer will operate in love and
support of one another. The sign of a true follower of
Christ is love. Love, in turn, produces unity.

> *By this shall all men know that ye are my*
> *disciples, if ye have love one to another. (John*
> *13:35)*

Since God and Christ are love, the apostolic spirit
compels believers to work together in unity. The unity
produced through the apostolic spirit sets the stage for
the manifestation of power in the Church.

2. **Power** – The assembly walking under an apostolic spirit will be a place of healing, deliverance, and salvation. The miraculous will be seen daily in the life of that church. The least to the greatest among the people will demonstrate the power of God in healing the sick, casting out of devils, and effective evangelism.

> *And these signs shall follow them that believe; In my name shall they cast out devils; they shall speak with new tongues; They shall take up serpents; and if they drink any deadly thing, it shall not hurt them; they shall lay hands on the sick, and they shall recover. (Mark 16:17-18)*

3. **Expansion of the Kingdom of God** – After unity and power, the church flowing in the apostolic spirit will cause expansion in the Kingdom. The assembly will grow, not because of other believers coming to fellowship. It will grow because souls will be added daily to the Kingdom because of the power and love expressed. In turn, the assembly will be a force in its city, county, and state because of the apostolic spirit.

> *And the Lord added to the church daily such as should be saved. (Acts 2:47b)*

The apostolic spirit is something that every fellowship of believers should seek for. The early Church had it and the Lord prospered them. If we possess it, we will see the miraculous of the Books of Acts today. In addition, the Kingdom of God will advance. Now that we have discussed the different aspects of apostleship, we have created a diagram showing the different levels in apostleship. The apostolic progression from the apostolic gift to the apostolic spirit is comparable to a flight of steps. The only way to go higher, one has to climb the steps. If the Church appreciates the apostolic gift, apostolic anointing, and apostolic office, we will experience the apostolic spirit in our day.

The apostolic spirit will only manifest as the apostleship of the believers and apostles is accepted and received. The apostolic spirit is something the entire Church is to possess.

Apostolic Ascension Diagram

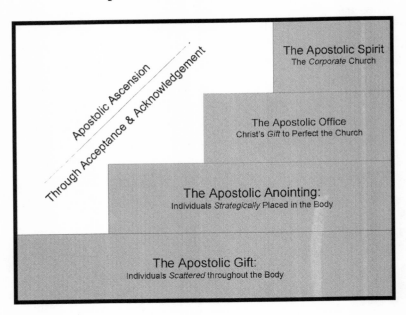

The illustration of the steps provides the basis for a general truth concerning the apostolic. The Church is supposed to be an apostolic Church. It is to reflect Christ's nature and power. The Church cannot become an apostolic Church without the ministry of the apostles and the apostolic anointing.

As the Church embraces (accepts and acknowledges) each manifestation of the apostolic, it moves a step closer to becoming apostolic corporately, culminating with the Church fulfilling its commission given by Christ to the apostles.

Guidelines for Judging the Apostolic

One of the major facets of understanding apostleship is to discern when something is not apostolic. Judging the apostolic can be a tough task at times. Nevertheless, there are guidelines to help us as we strive to receive those with this gift and anointing. We need the apostolic in the Church, but some of us have lost faith in the apostolic gift and ministry.

If you are unsure as to what and who is apostolic, there are certain questions you can ask yourself.

We must understand that God is the giver of the apostolic grace. We do not need to be afraid, but discerning. Even if we have heard or seen individuals misrepresent the apostolic office and gift, we should not allow the enemy to steal a blessing from us. God may be trying to even birth an apostolic gift in you or send someone with this anointing for your benefit.

Is the individual humble? Those with an apostolic calling and gift will be humble. They will know that without God, they can do nothing. They will consistently turn the people's attention to Christ and not themselves.

> *But God forbid that I should glory, save in the cross of our Lord Jesus Christ, by whom the world is crucified unto me, and I unto the world. (Galatians 6:14)*

Conversely, do not be quick to say someone does not have this gift or anointing because of character flaws. Apostles and apostolic individuals grow in grace and character as other believers.

Is their doctrine sound and full of wisdom? Those with an apostolic gift (ministers or not) will have a clear understanding of the scriptures. They will be able to present the word of God with clarity. They will continue to develop their doctrine because they respect God and His word. They desire that all understand God's truth through the scriptures

On the other hand, there are apostolic individuals who have a valid gift, but they are in the middle of God's process of perfecting. They still may be on the potter's wheel. Some may try to operate in this anointing and gift before time. This may contribute to elementary or erroneous doctrine.

Do they follow leadership? Apostolic individuals will respect and follow leadership. Christ came in submission to the Father. Apostolic individuals will support leadership. They know that this is pleasing to Christ.

Individuals who find it hard to follow leadership may not have sat at the foot of Christ. One sign of an apostolic call is that they follow Christ. To follow Christ is to follow His example. He ministered in submission to the Father. The apostolic individual will minister in subjection to leadership.

Is there a manifestation of authority and power in the Spirit of God? Part of the apostolic call is the working of the miraculous power of God. Any individual claiming an apostolic gift or anointing should show some level of giftedness by the Spirit and results in ministering. There should be testimonies of salvation, healing, and deliverance from others concerning them.

Is there confirmation of the apostolic call or gift? God is not the author of confusion. He does not work against Himself. He will not give a gift or calling without providing some form of confirmation in the Body. Even if your gift is not specifically stated, there will be a recognition of the grace that is upon your life. However, if an individual is claiming the apostolic office, there will be confirmation (usually by elders and apostles) of the ministry.

Shun away from individuals claiming an apostolic call and no one else knows about it. Usually, these individuals are self-willed. They demonstrate little power. Oftentimes, they are not faithful or accountable to anyone.

8

False Apostles

There is still much to be learned about the apostolic office. However, understanding comes with responsibility. The Church has to stand against deception. The scriptures are clear that the number of false ministers will increase as the end of this age approaches. Not every individual preaching in the name of the Lord is His servant.

The enemy seeks to destroy the work of God in the earth through imitation. Therefore, the enemy sets his false ministers in the Church to undermine the work of God's chosen vessels. False ministers are here, but the saints are not to be afraid of falling into deception. False ministers provide a service to the Church. How?

For there must be also heresies among you, that they which are approved may be made manifest among you. (I Corinthians 11:19)

When Paul used the word heresies, he was speaking of divisions and those that caused them. False ministers

97

seek to keep the Church in perpetual dissension and division. Their ministries put enmity between believers with the intent to create a following for themselves.

The answer to "How do false ministers provide a service to the Church?" seems non-existent. However, the statement of Paul provides a simple explanation. False ministers help us to recognize true ministers of God. Paul said that there must be heresies (and those that cause them) among you so that those who are approved (right, true, anointed, etc.) might be made visible.

The ministries of false ministers demonstrate to the Church the improper way to minister. Therefore, when true ministry is in operation, it can be received without fear.

Recognizing False Ministers

We cannot end our discussion of apostles without discussing false apostles. Before examining false apostles exclusively, it is imperative that we are able to recognize the characteristics of any false minister (or layman). Jesus gave this warning concerning false ministers.

> *Beware of false prophets, which come to you in sheep's clothing, but inwardly they are ravening wolves. Ye shall know them by their fruits. Do men gather grapes of thorns, or figs of thistles? Even so every good tree bringeth forth good fruit; but a corrupt tree bringeth forth evil fruit. A good tree cannot bring forth evil fruit, neither can a corrupt tree bring forth*

good fruit. Every tree that bringeth not forth good fruit is hewn down, and cast into the fire. Wherefore by their fruits ye shall know them. (Matthew 7:15-20)

One true way to recognize false ministers is by the fruit that they bear. Fruit refers to their lifestyles and not their ministries. Moreover, not everyone that is false calls himself an apostle or prophet.

Though false apostles exist, there are also false evangelists, pastors, and teachers. Regardless of the title that a false minister has, he (or she) will exhibit the following characteristics.

They preach that godliness is gain. Godliness to false ministers means prosperity and healing. They seldom teach against sin. They promote serving God for what you can get.

If any man teach otherwise, and consent not to wholesome words, even the words of our Lord Jesus Christ, and to the doctrine which is according to godliness; He is proud, knowing nothing, but doting about questions and strifes of words, whereof cometh envy, strife, railings, evil surmisings, perverse disputings of men of corrupt minds, and destitute of the truth, supposing that gain is godliness: from such withdraw thyself.   (I Timothy 6:3-5)

They only teach that you belong to God and should have the best. They promote the concept that God only wants you blessed, without declaring that God also wants character, integrity, and holiness in His people.

Their doctrine focuses on the miraculous work of God and His blessings, exclusively. They promote God's blessing, rather than God and His Christ. They teach individuals how to prosper in God without living for Him.

They were once servants of God. Many false ministers have genuine conversion experiences. They entered ministry by the call of God. However, consistent rebellion, sin, pride, and greed caused them to error from the truth.

> *For if after they have escaped the pollutions of the world through the knowledge of the Lord and Saviour Jesus Christ, they are again entangled therein, and overcome, the latter end is worse with them than the beginning. For it had been better for them not to have known the way of righteousness, than, after they have known it, to turn from the holy commandment delivered unto them. But it is happened unto them according to the true proverb, the dog is turned to his own vomit again; and the sow that was washed to her wallowing in the mire. (II Peter 2:20-22)*

Peter wrote that false ministers did escape the pollutions of the world by Christ. However, they returned to their sins and filthy ways. Consequently, Peter added, they are worse than they were before their initial conversion. It serves as a warning to every minister. If the love of money, pride, and sin are not rejected, the road to becoming an enemy of God becomes inevitable.

100

Recognizing False Apostles

False apostles will demonstrate the same behavior as other false ministers. However, there will be certain traits that readily visible in false prophetic ministers.

They minister for money. False apostles will always include money in their ministry. No matter the topic or subject, it will end up on money. They will twist scriptures to manipulate the people into giving to them. Remember:

NO APOSTLE OF SCRIPTURE EVER PREACHED FOR MONEY.

They will tell you to give in order to "seal" the prophetic words that they speak. We should give to ministers that have blessed us, but it should never be by their request.

We can bless those that have blessed us spiritually. In the scriptures, they would bless the apostle because of the spiritual impartation. They gave because they wanted to, not because the apostle demanded it.

They operate in false authority. False apostles do not operate in godly authority. They establish their own authority in the Body of Christ. They disguise their wickedness by first appearing as true apostles.

> *For such are false apostles, deceitful workers, transforming themselves into the apostles of Christ. And no marvel; for Satan himself is transformed into an angel of light. Therefore*

101

it is no great thing if his ministers also be transformed as the ministers of righteousness; whose end shall be according to their works. (II Corinthians 11:13-15)

Paul stated that those who are false would resemble those who are true. However, once they have gained some respect, they will attack other leaders. The false apostles and leaders of Paul's day tried to defame him and establish their own authority in the churches. False apostles use this tactic today. Through the defamation of others, they exalt their personal ministries.

They twist the scriptures. Another tactic used is misinterpretation of scripture to establish authority. They find scriptures that refer to apostolic authority and claim it for themselves. They scare believers into thinking that because they are apostles, they are superior to others.

True apostles will be humble. They will not promote their personal ministries. The authority that they operate in is backed by the power of God and recognized in the Church.

They operate in counterfeit gifts. False apostles minister with the wrong motives. Therefore, the Spirit of God withdraws Himself from their ministries. Since false apostles do not recognize the withdrawal of God, they strive to operate in gifts to validate the ministry. They begin to rely on their own human spirit and help from demonic influence to appear spiritual. This happened to King Saul.

> *But the Spirit of the Lord departed from Saul, and an evil spirit from the Lord troubled him. (I Samuel 16:14)*

> *And it came to pass on the morrow, that the evil spirit from God came upon Saul, and he prophesied in the midst of the house: and David played with his hand, as at other times: and there was a javelin in Saul's hand. (I Samuel 18:10)*

Because of Saul's continual rebellion, the Spirit of God departed from him. An evil spirit replaced God's Spirit. When the evil spirit came upon him, he prophesied. His prophecy came from the wrong source. This eventually happens to false apostles. The Holy Spirit leaves and they use demonic influence to still function.

They prophesy lies from their imaginations. False apostles will pretend to have a valid prophetic gift. They will make up lofty prophetic utterances. They will seem very spiritual, but oftentimes vague in content.

> *I have heard what the prophets said, that prophesy lies in my name, saying, I have dreamed, I have dreamed. How long shall this be in the heart of the prophets that prophesy lies? yea, they are prophets of the deceit of their own heart. (Jeremiah 23:25-26)*

They will give prophecies based upon someone's outer appearance and expression. In addition, they prophesy their own desires. Conversely, because a prophetic word may seem vague, it does not mean it is not from the Lord. The Lord may speak a word in part that the hearer would be drawn into seeking the Lord for clarity.

They possess a controlling spirit. False apostles will use manipulation to gain followers. Once people begin to follow them, they scare the individuals into staying. They tell individuals that if they leave, God will not be pleased and the like. In addition, the apostle will try to control the people's personal lives. By using false authority, they will tell people who they can marry and where to work. False apostles operate in a similar fashion to cult leaders.

Though false apostles and ministers exist, believers are not to walk in fear. However, Christians have to be able to learn to recognize false ministers. In addition, the presence of false ministers should give believers a greater appreciation for godly leaders and ministries within the Church.

About the Author

Prophet Evans was called into the ministry at the age of 19. He is an associate minister at Mt. Zion C.O.G.I.C. located in Camden, NC where his pastor is the Elder Glenn Sawyer. He serves on the administrative staff and advisory board.

Among his accomplishments, Prophet Evans has received a Diploma from Harvester's Christian Fellowship School of Ministry. He has authored various books and teaching resources. In addition, he is a gifted lyricist and composer who has published various music books.

He is the founder of Kingdom Builders International Ministries. A ministry dedicated to promoting maturity, unity, and holiness in the Body of Christ. He is the founder and president of Kingdom Builders International Ministries School of Ministry located in Kenya, East Africa. He is also the founder of Kingdom Builders Ministerial Alliance located in various parts of the world.

He has been the featured speaker at various functions, including youth, men, women, and consecration services. He ministers under a precise prophetic anointing and an apostolic anointing that represents the heart of the Father.

He and his family reside in Elizabeth City, North Carolina, from which he travels ministering the word of the Lord.

105

Appendix

The ministry of the apostle and gifts of the Spirit are a source of controversy and excitement. This appendix lists some popular passages of scriptures concerning ministries and gifts. These are given to inspire others to research this topic.

The Outpouring of the Spirit (Acts 2:17-18)

17. And it shall come to pass in the last days, saith God, I will pour out of my Spirit upon all flesh: and your sons and your daughters shall prophesy, and your young men shall see visions, and your old men shall dream dreams:

18. And on my servants and on my handmaidens I will pour out in those days of my Spirit; and they shall prophesy:

The Nine Gifts of the Spirit (I Corinthians 12:4-11)

4. Now there are diversities of gifts, but the same Spirit.

5. And there are differences of administrations, but the same Lord.

6. And there are diversities of operations, but it is the same God which worketh all in all.

7. But the manifestation of the Spirit is given to every man to profit withal.

8. For to one is given by the Spirit the word of wisdom; to another the word of knowledge by the same Spirit;

9. To another faith by the same Spirit; to another the gifts of healing by the same Spirit;

10. To another the working of miracles; to another prophecy; to another discerning of spirits; to another divers kinds of tongues; to another the interpretation of tongues:

11. But all these worketh that one and the selfsame Spirit, dividing to every man severally as he will.

The Setting of Gifts in the Church (I Corinthians 12:27-28)

27. Now ye are the body of Christ, and members in particular.

28. And God hath set some in the church, first apostles, secondarily prophets, thirdly teachers, after that miracles, then gifts of healings, helps, governments, diversities of tongues.

The Gift of Tongues versus Prophecy (I Corinthians 14:1-9)

1. Follow after charity, and desire spiritual gifts, but rather that ye may prophesy.

2. For he that speaketh in an unknown tongue speaketh not unto men, but unto God: for no man understandeth him; howbeit in the spirit he speaketh mysteries.

3. But he that prophesieth speaketh unto men to edification, and exhortation, and comfort.

4. He that speaketh in an unknown tongue edifieth himself; but he that prophesieth edifieth the church.

5. I would that ye all spake with tongues; but rather that ye prophesied: for greater is he that prophesieth than he that speaketh with tongues, except he interpret, that the church may receive edifying.

6. Now, brethren, if I come unto you speaking with tongues, what shall I profit you, except I shall speak to you either by revelation, or by knowledge, or by prophesying, or by doctrine?

7. And even things without life giving sound, whether pipe or harp, except they give a distinction in the sounds, how shall it be known what is piped or harped?

8. For if the trumpet give an uncertain sound, who shall prepare himself to the battle?

9. So likewise ye, except ye utter by the tongue words easy to be understood, how shall it be known what is spoken? for ye shall speak into the air.

Protocol for Tongues and Prophecy (I Corinthians 14:27-33)

27. If any man speak in an unknown tongue, let it be by two, or at the most by three, and that by course; and let one interpret.

28. But if there be no interpreter, let him keep silence in the church; and let him speak to himself, and to God.

29. Let the prophets speak two or three, and let the other judge.

30. If any thing be revealed to another that sitteth by, let the first hold his peace.

31. For ye may all prophesy one by one, that all may learn, and all may be comforted.

32. And the spirits of the prophets are subject to the prophets.

33. For God is not the author of confusion, but of peace, as in all churches of the saints.

Other Ministries/Gifts of the Spirit (Romans 12:4-8)

4. For as we have many members in one body, and all members have not the same office:

5. So we, being many, are one body in Christ, and every one members one of another.

6. Having then gifts differing according to the grace that is given to us, whether prophecy, let us prophesy according to the proportion of faith;

7. Or ministry, let us wait on our ministering: or he that teacheth, on teaching;

8. Or he that exhorteth, on exhortation: he that giveth, let him do it with simplicity; he that ruleth, with diligence; he that sheweth mercy, with cheerfulness.

The Ministry Gifts and Purpose (Ephesians 4:11-15)

11. And he gave some, apostles; and some, prophets; and some, evangelists; and some, pastors and teachers;

12. For the perfecting of the saints, for the work of the ministry, for the edifying of the body of Christ:

13. Till we all come in the unity of the faith, and of the knowledge of the Son of God, unto a perfect man, unto the measure of the stature of the fulness of Christ:

14. That we henceforth be no more children, tossed to and fro, and carried about with every wind of doctrine, by the sleight of men, and cunning craftiness, whereby they lie in wait to deceive;

15. But speaking the truth in love, may grow up into him in all things, which is the head, even Christ:

Bibliography

Evans, Roderick L. *No Other Foundation.* Writers Club Press. Lincoln, NE, c2003

Lockman Foundation. *Comparative Study Bible.* Zondervan Publishing House. Grand Rapids, MI, c1984

Other Books from Kingdom Builders International Ministries

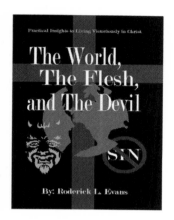

The World, The Flesh, and The Devil provides guidelines for overcoming the three battlegrounds every Christian faces—the world, the flesh, and the devil. Learn how you can walk in the power of God. Discover how you, too, can live victoriously in Christ.

When Christ came, the scriptures stated that the "Word Was Made Flesh." This reveals to us that in Christ, the proper way to see God was presented in His life. His lifestyle became a demonstration of the law of God and of the character of God in the earth. When we understand how the principles of Christ and the personality of Christ operate together, we will grow in our understanding of His Word and His ways.

In this book, we will bring clarity to the roles of the apostles and prophets in the New Testament Church. In addition, we will explain with simplicity the apostolic and the prophetic anointing. It is our prayer that believers will recognize the operation of them in their lives and in the lives of others. We can be confident that God is still using His people in these last days.

If you would like to purchase these books, to see a full listing of music, teachings, and other ministry resources, and/or to learn more about Kingdom Builders International Ministries, please visit our website at www.kbpublications.net

Other Books from Kingdom Builders International Ministries

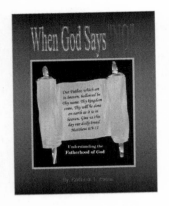

In the pages of this book, we want to explore reasons why God's answer to us is not always right in our eyes. We will examine causes for the Lord denying the request of our hearts. In addition, we will learn how God's seemingly unfavorable response to us in certain requests is actually a demonstration of His love, care, and concern for us. This will lead us to a greater understanding of the Fatherhood of God in the life of the believer.

This book brings clarity to the role of the prophet in the New Testament Church. In addition, it explores the prophetic person and the prophetic anointing. It is our prayer that believers will recognize the operation of the prophetic office and gift in the Church.

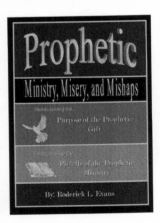

The focus of this book is to bring clarity and understanding to the gift of prophecy. Many lives have been negatively influenced. **Misery** was a product of these **Mishaps** in ministry. This information will help individuals to recognize the operation of the gift of the prophecy in their lives and in the lives of others. It is our hope that believers will develop a greater respect and appreciation for the inspiration, revelation, and power of the Holy Spirit in the Body of Christ.

If you would like to purchase these books, to see a full listing of music, teachings, and other ministry resources, and/or to learn more about Kingdom Builders International Ministries, please visit our website at www.kbpublications.net

Other Books from Kingdom Builders International Ministries

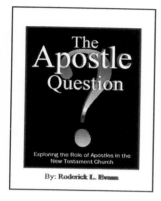

The focus of this book is to bring clarity and understanding to the role of the apostle in the Church. Sound biblical answers to questions concerning the function of the apostle are answered. This information will help individuals to recognize the operations of this anointing in their lives and in the lives of others. It is our hope that believers will develop a greater respect and acceptance of the apostolic office and gift.

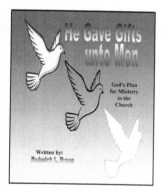

Ministry is a valuable part of the Kingdom. God anoints individuals in the Church with ministries and gifts to glorify Him. However, as the day of the Lord hastens, we find many believers entering into ministry with wrong motives. In addition, others are pursuing gifts for their own personal gain. We are members of the body of Christ. God places us in the Body to minister and serve one another. This book will give believers a pure perspective for ministry.

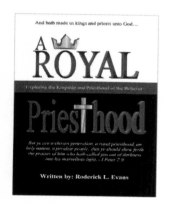

The believer receives kingship and priesthood through Jesus. To have a people of a royal priesthood has always been a part of God's plan for His people. It was His desire for the children of Israel, yet He developed this desire in the believers. In the pages of this book, we will bring clarity to the believers as the royal priesthood.

If you would like to purchase these books, to see a full listing of music, teachings, and other ministry resources, and/or to learn more about Kingdom Builders International Ministries, please visit our website at www.kbpublications.net

Other Books from Kingdom Builders International Ministries

How do you handle your failures? Do you allow them to paralyze your personal growth and happiness? Or, do you learn from them? The Bible contains numerous accounts of individuals who failed in their relationship with Him. Yet, this did not prevent them from doing great things for Him. Throughout the pages of this book, we will examine the failures and ultimate successes of biblical characters. Their examples provide hope and strength for the Christian today.

When Jesus came, He told us that the Kingdom of God was at hand, upon us, and is coming. If He made so many references to the Kingdom of God, it is then our responsibility to learn how to live in the Kingdom of God. We must live as if we are a part of the Kingdom of God. It is only the only way we can prosper and live in victory; for the Scriptures say that our citizenship is in heaven (Philippians 3:20). We are a part of the Kingdom of God now and will be partakers of the glory of the Kingdom of God at Christ's return. Rejoice and be glad for the Kingdom of heaven belongs to you.

In this book, we will discuss the gifts and ministries of the Spirit of God, their functions, and how to recognize them in operation. God gives the Church gifts to benefit everyone. The purpose of the gifts is not make us spiritual, but to help us to serve and minister to one another in love. The operation of the Spirit of God and His gifts/ministries among believers testifies to the presence of God in the Church.

If you would like to purchase these books, to see a full listing of music, teachings, and other ministry resources, and/or to learn more about Kingdom Builders International Ministries, please visit our website at www.kbpublications.net

6543037R0

Made in the USA
Lexington, KY
29 August 2010